The role of Fostering for Adoption in achieving early permanence for children

Elaine Dibben and Viv Howorth

coram centre for early permanence

coramBAAF ADOPTION & FOSTERING ACADEMY

Published by
CoramBAAF Adoption and Fostering Academy
41 Brunswick Square
London WC1N 1AZ
www.corambaaf.org.uk

Coram Academy Limited, registered as a company limited by guarantee in England and Wales number 9697712, part of the Coram group, charity number 312278

British Library Cataloguing in Publication Data
A catalogue record for this book is available from the British Library

ISBN 978 1 910039 61 8

Project management by Jo Francis, CoramBAAF
Designed and typeset by Helen Joubert Design
Printed in Great Britain by the Lavenham Press

Contents

Acknowledgements

We are grateful to Coram for commissioning this Good Practice Guide as part of their Early Permanence Project, funded by the DfE Practice Improvement Fund, and for their interest and encouragement in its development.

We are indebted to the Fostering for Adoption (FfA) adopters who responded to our request to complete questionnaires about their experiences. Their accounts have brought to life the joys and challenges of FfA placements for those who take this route to creating their families.

We would also like to thank social work colleagues who attended the focus groups, particularly those who then responded to our requests to circulate questionnaires and provide information about their existing policies, and agreed to us sharing their tools and proformas.

We were greatly helped by Lindy Wooton (CCS Adoption), Dawn May (Northamptonshire County Council), Jan Owen (Somerset County Council) Colette Jones (Chester West and Cheshire Council) and Kate Knowles (Caritas Care), who read drafts of this book and gave feedback, and Jeanne Kaniuk (Coram) and John Simmonds (CoramBAAF) for acting as sounding boards and providing challenges to us on determining good practice in this area. We would also like to thank Kathy s'Jacob and Sarah Coldrick (AFA Cymru) for their assistance in providing information about Foster to Adopt in Wales. Many thanks also to the Department for Education and their legal adviser for their contribution.

We are also grateful to Essex County Council, Northamptonshire County Council, CCS Adoption, Families for Children, Cornwall Council and Leeds City Council for sharing materials that they have developed and which will benefit other agencies.

Finally, we would like to thank Jo Francis (CoramBAAF Publications) and Shaila Shah for their encouragement and assistance with proofreading and support in bringing together the final product.

Notes about the authors

Elaine Dibben started her social work career in residential social work and qualified in 1988. She has over 25 years' experience of working in adoption and fostering in local authority and voluntary adoption agency settings. She joined BAAF in 2004 to become manager of the Independent Review Mechanism, which she set up and ran until 2009, when she moved to take on a wider role in BAAF as a trainer consultant.

She is currently an Adoption Development Consultant for CoramBAAF, alongside acting as a Panel Chair for both adoption and fostering panels.

She currently sits on the National Recruitment and Matching Forum, a sub-group of the Adoption Leadership Board, and the Early Permanence Working Group established by the DfE in 2016. She has written several books and Good Practice Guides published by BAAF/CoramBAAF, including *Adoption by Foster Carers* (2016) with Viv Howorth, *Completing a Child's Permanence Report* (2014), *Parent and Child Fostering*, with Paul Adams (2011), *Preparing to Adopt* (2014), with Eileen Fursland and Nicky Probert, and *Undertaking an Adoption Assessment in England* (2010) (third edition 2017). She has also written online guides on adoption for Community Care Inform in 2016/17. She lives in Oxfordshire with her husband, Steve.

Viv Howorth commenced her social work career in residential settings in the North West of England and then continued her professional career as a qualified worker in South Yorkshire. She has 30 years' experience of working in children and families teams and of fostering and adoption work.

In 2004, Viv joined BAAF as a trainer consultant in Yorkshire and Humber and was BAAF Northern Regional Director between 2012 and 2014.

Viv has now returned to social work practice as a part-time adoption social worker and is also continuing independent work, including chairing adoption panels and some training. In 2016, she co-authored the Good Practice Guide, *Adoption by Foster Carers,* with Elaine Dibben. Viv lives in South Yorkshire.

FOREWORD

I am delighted to introduce *The Role of Fostering for Adoption in Achieving Early Permanence for Children*, a comprehensive update designed to inspire confident and informed delivery.

Practice has advanced since the introduction of Fostering for Adoption provisions in legislation in 2014, but there is more to do and young children, where adoption is the most likely outcome, still suffer the adverse impact of multiple carers and uncertainty.

We hope that this guidance supports agencies to develop assured and confident approaches that will maximise outcomes for children in their developmental timeline.

The guidance presents a clear exposition of early permanence, concurrent planning and Fostering for Adoption as it is now, the legal backdrop, recent case scenarios, practice tips, and the roles and duties of agencies in relation to each of the parties. The information is expected to be a practice aid and agency resource, strengthening delivery strategies as part of service development.

This guidance is commissioned by the Coram Centre for Early Permanence, funded by the DfE as part of its Practice Improvement Fund programme and is published by CoramBAAF following extensive consultation through sector engagement.

We are grateful for the significant support of all agencies that contributed to the consultations and focus groups that informed this guidance.

Dr Carol Homden, CBE
Chief Executive, Coram

Chapter 1
Introduction

Fostering for Adoption (FfA) is a recently introduced route to providing permanence for a child who cannot live with their birth family. Prior to FfA being introduced, the majority of children who were first placed for adoption were placed with short-term foster carers once they were removed from their birth family, and remained in foster care till the placement order was made. The exception to this was a small number of children who were placed through specialist schemes with concurrent carers who would foster them whilst a rehabilitation plan was being attempted; if this was not successful, the carers would go on to adopt the children. Whilst the number of children benefitting from concurrent planning schemes was small, the benefits to the children were recognised as significant – namely, a reduction in the number of moves and delays these babies and young children experienced prior to being placed in their permanent home, and the formation of earlier attachments between the child and their permanent carers.

However, the complexities of concurrent planning meant that there was little increase in the number of children being placed through this route. This led to the development of FfA, which has built on the successes of concurrency and is also seen to open up the possibility of achieving early permanence to a greater number of children.

THE BEGINNINGS OF FfA LEGISLATION AND PRACTICE GUIDANCE

In 2012, the Department for Education (DfE) consultation, *Adoption and Fostering: Tackling Delay*, introduced the concept of FfA as a new route to achieving early permanence for children. An update to the *Children Act 1989 Guidance and Regulations Volume 2: Care Planning, Placement and Case Review* (DfE, 2013) on 'Temporary approval of prospective adopters as foster carers' was published in May 2013 alongside the Adoption Statutory Guidance (published in July 2013).

Practice guidance on FfA was commissioned from BAAF (now CoramBAAF) by the Coram Centre for Early Permanence, and published in June 2013 (Coram and BAAF, 2013). This guidance was seen as 'a comprehensive first step towards understanding the role that Fostering for Adoption may play in the future and a useful voluntary aid to this emerging area of adoption policy and practice'. It explained 'where

Fostering for Adoption fits into the changing landscape of delivery, the practice implications, and how it shares the same principles of early permanence as concurrent planning'. We have re-used or adapted sections of this original guide where they are still relevant.

There was always an intention that that guidance would be reviewed as policy and practice developed, and that has led to this guide being commissioned from CoramBAAF by Coram as part of their work on early permanence, supported by the DfE Practice and Improvement Fund. The guide's focus is on England and Wales, although the material will be of interest more widely.

Since the original guidance was written, the Children and Families Act 2014 in England has introduced legislation requiring local authorities to consider FfA as part of their care planning for permanence for a child, and provided Statutory Guidance, *Early Permanence Placements and Approval of Prospective Adopters as Foster Carers*, in July 2014. This was later subsumed into the Volume 2 *Care Planning, Placement and Review* statutory guidance issued in 2015. Draft Adoption Statutory Guidance was also published for consultation in 2014 but has not been finalised; where the 2014 version contains updated information that is relevant to this book, that text has been used here.

USE OF FOCUS GROUPS AND QUESTIONNAIRES

In writing this guide, we were aware that practice around FfA, dual approval care and concurrent planning, as pathways to pursue early permanence for children in care who may not be able to return to their birth family, has been developing over time. Prior to writing the guide, we held three focus groups in London, Doncaster and Bridgewater, attended by 36 local authorities and 10 voluntary adoption agencies (VAAs) to hear about and learn from these agencies about their experiences, the developments they were making in this area of practice, the challenges they were facing, and the ways to overcome these. Some agencies were working together within consortia or, looking forward, within regional adoption agencies (RAAs) to develop their processes; some were part of the Coram Early Permanence subscription service; and others were just working within their own agency to progress FfA and early permanence. Their insights have helped to inform this guide.

In addition, we asked agencies to nominate some families who had adopted through the FfA route to complete a questionnaire about their experiences; in fact, some of those who contacted us had adopted following a concurrent planning placement. Their accounts show how their motivation to adopt developed into an understanding of the benefits to children of early permanence placements, and evidence their strong support for the use of these placements. They also offer some useful insights into their experiences of providing the fostering placement, give some powerful evidence about the impact on children of contact arrangements, and highlight issues around adoption support for families who adopt through this route. We have used quotes from these questionnaires throughout the book (under coded names), and summaries of the families' situations are given in Appendix 1 to provide context.

> *It's the most rewarding thing to do yet it's also a rollercoaster of a ride. It's not always easy, sometimes feeling as if it's never going to happen, but you need to focus and remember that you're doing it because it's the best thing for the child, not for you. As adults, we have the capabilities to cope with loss much better than a child can and it's only right that as adults we take the risks, not the child.* (FfA8)

TERMINOLOGY AND REMIT OF THIS GUIDE

During our focus group discussions and in some of the responses from FfA and concurrent carers, we recognised that although current statutory guidance sets out a distinction between concurrent placements and FfA, the experience of agencies is that it is not possible to pre-empt the outcome of care proceedings, even with cases that are initially considered to be very "straightforward". Some agencies have therefore chosen to use the term "early permanence" for all the placements they make through FfA using temporary approval through Reg. 25a or dual approval, and for their concurrent planning placements, and will highlight to prospective carers that every early placement carries a level of risk for the prospective carers that the child may return to the care of a birth family member. These different routes to early permanence are explained further in the next chapter.

When FfA was first introduced, there was a lack of understanding about this new concept, particularly around the fostering aspect of the role, and it was reported that some courts and legal professionals confused this concept with foster carers who wanted to adopt a child for whom they were already caring. Adoption by carers does provide another route to permanence for children of all ages, and it was recommended by Dibben and Howorth (2016) that it is an opportunity that could be extended to a wider number of children in care, but it is not covered here.

WHAT THIS BOOK COVERS

In this guide, we set out the development of FfA as a route to early permanence and explore current best policy and practice.

- Chapter 2 explores the historical development of FfA as a route to early permanence.
- Chapter 3 sets out the legal requirements on local authorities when they are care planning for children and identifying FfA carers, and acknowledges the differences between legislation and guidance in England and Wales.
- Chapter 4 looks at which children will benefit from an FfA placement and gives case examples from local authority experience.
- Chapter 5 looks at how practice has been developing and what can lead to good practice in the care planning and placement of children in FfA placements. It also references or signposts agencies to models and resources that have been developed by agencies that have shared their materials with us.
- Chapter 6 covers the recruitment, preparation and assessment of FfA carers and highlights best practice, giving examples of local authority and VAA practice and sharing carers' accounts of their experiences.
- Chapter 7 explores how agencies and FfA carers can manage the period of the fostering placement whilst decisions are being made about the long-term future for the child, including situations where a child returns home. Accounts from FfA carers highlight some of the emotional impacts for them during this period. We examine the areas that need to be considered by agencies when setting up these placements and again highlight the best practice that is developing.
- Chapter 8 considers the further planning that is needed to progress the adoption match once authority to place has been given, in most cases following the conclusion of care proceedings, or once parental consent has been formalised, including the final consideration of the match and the role of the adoption panel.
- Chapter 9 addresses the post-match considerations and how agencies can support the prospective adoptive family through to the making of the adoption order, and what needs to be considered in the provision of adoption support.
- The conclusion sets out a summary of the main learning points for agencies to consider in their development of FfA so that they can identify the children who will most benefit from this route to early permanence and provide the right support to the families who are coming forward to offer an FfA placement.

  The Appendices provide relevant tools and information shared with us by several agencies that came to our focus groups, and give a brief outline of the families who have contributed their experiences to help inform adoption agencies and support future potential FfA carers.

Chapter 2
The development of Fostering for Adoption as a route to early permanence

Practice guidance on FfA (Coram and BAAF, 2013), highlights that the legal, policy and practice framework for adoption balances the rights and needs of the child's birth parents with those of the child.

Where the local authority's care and permanency planning process has led to the decision that adoption is the best plan for the child and where this is opposed by the birth parents, this framework has meant that the local authority was limited in what it could do to identify or make a placement other than preliminary family finding until it had the authorisation of the court through the making of a placement order. The child would usually be placed in temporary foster care until the placement order was made; a match was then identified and agreed by the matching panel; and the necessary information, advice, counselling of prospective adopters and birth parents, introductions to the child and support arrangements were completed.

However, the use of fostering placements with carers dually approved as adopters *and* foster carers providing a period of temporary care for the child until the court had made its decision about the appropriate order to secure the child's long-term future, has been possible and has been a route to early placement for a small number of children since the concurrent planning pilot projects of the late 1990s.

THE CONCURRENT PLANNING MODEL

Coram and BAAF (2013) set out how concurrent planning involves the identification and delivery of a detailed rehabilitation plan while the child is placed with carers who are approved for both fostering and adoption and who support that plan. Where the rehabilitation plan proves unsuccessful, once care proceedings and the placement order application are completed, the foster carers then go on to adopt the child.

Borthwick and Donnelly (2013) note that the original definition of concurrent planning as established by Linda Katz was: 'To work towards family reunification whilst at the same time establishing an alternative permanent plan'. They describe how the two plans for the child (Plan A and Plan B) would be developed and worked towards *at the same time* (i.e. concurrently).

- **Plan A** would involve a clearly defined time period during which a full assessment towards reunification would take place. The permanence options would also be explored during this time and decisions then reached to make recommendations to the court. Intensive work would be undertaken with the birth parent/s, including both assessment and support to establish whether the parent/s were able to demonstrate the required and agreed changes to their behaviours and/or lifestyle, within the child's timescale, to enable the child to return home. Workers would also be exploring the possibility of placing the child with other members of the birth family. It was expected that regular contact would be taking place between the child and family members so that workers could assess the quality of interactions and parents' abilities to change their behaviour, but also to support the child in establishing relationships with their parents. If rehabilitation became the outcome, this would be assisted by support of this ongoing relationship.
- **Plan B** would focus on providing a secure placement of the child with concurrent carers who would become the child's adopters if rehabilitation under Plan A was not possible.

The benefit to the child in these circumstances, where adoption then becomes the plan, is seen to be that the child's attachment relationship will not be disrupted (although Coram and BAAF (2013) noted that in the small number of cases where the child returns to the birth parents or another plan is agreed, the resulting disruption for the child would need to be addressed in careful planning for all those involved).

Coram and BAAF (2013) and others had questioned whether more could be done, building on the experiences of concurrent planning, to result in more children being placed with carers who could become their permanent carers within the current legislative, policy and practice frameworks for permanency planning. This question led to a proposal from BAAF to the DfE in 2012 to explore and expand the principles of concurrent planning to those cases where there was no active plan for rehabilitation. Following interest from the Secretary of State and the Prime Minister, the FfA model was developed as an alternative model to concurrent planning.

> *These new plans will see babies placed with approved adopters who will foster first, and help provide a stable home at a much earlier stage in a child's life. This way, we're trying our very best to avoid the disruption*

> *that can be so damaging to a child's development and so detrimental to their future well-being.*
>
> *I'm determined that we act now to give these children the very best start in life. These babies deserve what every child deserves: a permanent, secure and happy home environment to grow up in.*
>
> (David Cameron, Prime Minister, July 2012)

THE FOSTERING FOR ADOPTION (FfA) MODEL

The key principle in FfA is that the local authority will have already determined that the child is unlikely to return to the birth family and there is no active Plan A for rehabilitation, that it has considered and ruled out any potential family and friends carers, and that adoption is therefore likely to be their plan to achieve permanence for the child. The child is then placed in a fostering placement with FfA carers who would become the child's adopters if a placement order is made or parental consent given.

Whilst the conditions for making an FfA placement were seen to be different from concurrent planning, nevertheless it was also recognised early on that, in using FfA as a route to achieving early permanence for children, it was important that the learning from concurrent planning placements was considered.

Borthwick and Donnelly (2013, our emphasis), in their guide on concurrent planning, noted that:

> *As with concurrent planning, FfA aims to create continuity for carefully identified children, usually babies, who can be placed with foster carers who will go on to adopt them, if the court makes a placement order and the adoption agency agrees the match... As with concurrent planning, the dually approved carers will be expected to carry the burden of uncertainty during the fostering phase as there may be unexpected changes in the birth family situation and the child may be rehabilitated with a birth family member. The FfA carers will need to be assessed, properly prepared and supported in undertaking the fostering task. It is still for the court and only the court to authorise the plan for adoption when it makes a placement order.* ***FfA requires as much care, planning and resources as concurrent planning.***

As FfA placements have become part of the care planning process, these issues of care, planning and resources that were highlighted by Borthwick and Donnelly have been seen to be very relevant.

The process for dually approving concurrent carers, whilst meeting both fostering and adoption regulations, was achieved by some specialist schemes through a co-ordinated approach, but in some local authorities this led to the carers being assessed by more than one worker and being presented to both fostering and adoption panels to achieve their dual approval, and so a key element of the FfA proposal was to extend the options for dually approving FfA carers. In 2013, the Government therefore introduced Reg. 25a into the Care Planning, Placement and Case Review (England) Regulations 2010, which provided for:

> *The temporary approval of prospective adopters as foster carers for a named child where the child's local authority are satisfied that placement with that person is the most appropriate placement for the child and is in his or her best interests.*

There was an expectation set out in statutory guidance that agencies would inform adopters about this new route of FfA during assessment and provide information on what it would mean for them.

The statutory guidance set out the two routes available for FfA:

- **dual approval**, where the agency would 'approve the adopter as a foster carer under the Fostering Services (England) Regulations 2011 (FSR 2011) so that they could foster any child for whom FfA is suitable' *or*
- **temporary approval**, where the agency would 'note the prospective adopter's interest... and assess and approve the prospective adopter when there is a specific child for whom they would be a suitable FfA placement' (DfE, 2013a, 2.12).

There was an expectation that adopters' interest in offering an FfA placement would be made known to other agencies through 'sharing with local consortia or commissioning arrangements with VAAs and other local authorities' (DfE, 2013a, 2.13).

Statutory Guidance (DfE, 2013a) acknowledged that FfA was building on the experiences of concurrent planning and the principle of early permanence (DfE, 2013a, 2.7) and gave the following explanations for the model that identified when FfA should be used. (References to approved carers refer to carers who are dually approved or who have been given temporary approval through Reg. 25A for a specific child):

> ***Fostering for Adoption*** *(FfA) is about those cases where a child is placed with carers who are both approved adopters and approved foster carers. It is a fostering placement under the Children Act 1989 but which may lead to adoption by those foster carers, where it is decided that adoption is the plan for the child and either the court agrees to make a placement order, or parental consent to adoption is given. The advantage of this type of placement is that the child will be able to be placed much earlier with foster carers who are likely to go on to become the child's adoptive family... There may be cases where a local authority identifies that, based on the evidence available and on its assessment of the case, the long-term permanence plan for a child is likely to be adoption... Local*

authorities must assess the appropriateness of placing the child in a FfA placement with dually approved carers on a case-by-case basis.

(DfE, 2013a, 2.5–2.6)

The guidance also refers to cases where 'the local authority may still be considering other outcomes for the child, and may still be attempting rehabilitation with family, but expects that adoption will become the plan should those alternatives not succeed' (2.5). In these circumstances, we would expect that a concurrent planning placement is more likely to be appropriate.

The guidance also identifies some distinctions between FfA and concurrent planning, particularly around the differing role of the FfA carers and their contact with the child's birth parents, noting that within the work being undertaken by the agency 'to help [the birth parents] to change their lifestyle and improve their parenting skills with the aim of enabling their child to return home to them', a dually approved *concurrent carer* will 'bring [the child] to regular supervised contact sessions with their parents and other relatives. In addition, the carer may spend time with the parents at both ends of contact sessions to update them on the child's progress. This enables a relationship to develop which is supportive to the parents.'

However, as we will discuss later in this guide, in practice this has not always been the case and the progression of individual cases has led to a blurring of these differing roles for FfA and concurrent planning carers in the arena of contact and meeting birth parents or relatives.

The Children and Families Act 2014 then introduced a new requirement on a local authority under s.22C of the Children Act 1989 to consider a placement with dually approved carers when it is considering adoption. This could be early in the care planning process – indeed, for some children it may even be part of pre-birth conferences – but can be considered again later in the process, for example, at the point when the agency decision-maker is making the decision that the child should be placed for adoption or a placement order is being applied for and the agency does not yet have authority to place the child for adoption through either a placement order or parental consent. This has introduced the use of FfA into the care planning process for children, with the intention of extending the benefits of such placements to a wider number of children.

Statutory Guidance, *Early Permanence Placements and Approval of Prospective Adopters as Foster Carers*, was published in July 2014 and then consolidated into *Volume 2: Care Planning, Placement and Case Review* in 2015 (DfE, 2015a), and sets out the circumstances in which concurrent planning or FfA placements can be considered:

- *where the local authority is trying to rehabilitate the child with the birth parents, there are no suitable family or friends carers and adoption is the best option for the child if rehabilitation does not succeed. This scenario is often known as concurrent planning,*
- *where the local authority has decided at the permanence planning stage that adoption should be the plan for the child. The permanence planning stage is normally by the second statutory review, which is held no later than four months after the child enters care, but can be much earlier. The local authority must be able to demonstrate to the agency decision-maker and the court why the child cannot return home, why the child has not been placed with family or friends, why no other permanence plan is appropriate for the child and why adoption is the right plan for the child,*
- *in cases where the birth parents have indicated that they are likely to consent to the child being placed for adoption, but have not yet consented,*
- *a section 22C(9B)(c) placement can also be made after the agency decision-maker has made the decision that the child should be placed for adoption, but does not yet have a placement order to place the child for adoption.*

(DfE, 2015, s.3.154)

USE OF FfA

The development of FfA has progressed since 2014 but there are still differences in the pace of development and therefore in how actively it is used. A number of agencies in our focus groups in October 2016 had placed between 15–20 children in FfA placements, whilst a few had made over 50 placements and others were still in single figures.

DfE statistics do not distinguish between figures for FfA and concurrent placements, but do show that 320 children were placed with a foster carer who is also an approved adopter for FfA or concurrent planning in the period ending March 2016, compared to 260 children in the period ending March 2015. This included a small number – between 20–30 – who were either relatives or "connected people", perhaps where these were being used for sibling placements. It could be assumed that some of the increase has arisen with the increased use of FfA placements.

There are no national figures being collected on the number of FfA or concurrent placements where children have returned to live with birth family or where there has been a placement disruption at the request of the FfA carer. We are not aware of any plans for this at present. In our focus groups, we were made aware of a small number of such cases.

Chapter 3
Fostering for Adoption legislation

Whilst both England and Wales have introduced the concept of using dually approved carers to offer continuity of care for children needing adoption beyond the route used in concurrent planning, there are significant differences in how they have been designed. In England, this route is known as Fostering for Adoption, whilst in Wales it is known as Fostering to Adopt. This chapter sets out the different approaches that have been taken.

ENGLAND

In order to ensure that placement for FfA is compliant with Article 8 (right to respect for one's private and family life) and Article 6 (right to a fair hearing) of the European Convention on Human Rights (ECHR), there are a number of steps that must be followed by the local authority as set out in Statutory Guidance:

- First, the local authority must decide that 'it is not consistent with the child's welfare and reasonably practicable for the child to live with his or her parents' and that alternative placement is needed (DfE, 2010, 22C(4)).
- Before making any decision, the authority must, as far as is reasonably practicable, ascertain the wishes and feelings of the parent or anyone with parental responsibility for the child and to take these into account (DfE, 2010, 22(4)).
- The local authority needs to explore whether there are any suitable family members or connected people with whom the child can be placed who can safeguard the child and meet his or her welfare needs (DfE, 2010, 22C(7)). In such cases, they would need to be approved as local authority foster carers under Section 24 if temporary approval is needed.
- The local authority should then consider whether an FfA placement under s.22C(9b) with a foster carer who is also an approved adopter is suitable before making a placement with a local authority/IFP foster carer.

The statutory and regulatory framework for Fostering for Adoption in England

(The following text has been adapted from the Care Planning, Placement and Case Review Guidance 2015)

Pre- or post-birth identification of a child who may be in need of adoption.

↓

Core assessment – Decision that the child needs to be looked after.

↓

Legal processes for the child to become looked after (s.31 or s.20).

↓

Care planning – explore a care plan of adoption (Regs. 5–7) including consideration of early placement (s.22C(9A)(a)).

↓

Placement – initiate an appropriate placement with a concurrent foster carer or FfA foster carer (s.22C(9B)(c)). NB: If not dually approved, then for Reg. 25a approval the Nominated Officer agrees to temporary approval of approved adopters as foster carers for the specific child.

↓

"Should be placed for adoption" decision made by agency decision-maker (or care plan for adoption not agreed).

↓

Parental consent witnessed/care order and placement order made (or child returns to birth family following change of care plan).

↓

Match presented to the adoption panel.

↓

Agency decision-maker agrees the match and the placement becomes an adoption placement.

- Agreement to making a s.22C placement must be given by a Nominated Officer who is appointed by the Director of Children's Services. It is expected that that person will be a social worker with a good understanding of care planning, including adoption and fostering. They could be the adoption agency decision-maker (DfE, 2013, 13).

  CoramBAAF provides a proforma (as part of the PAR) for both the approval of a s.22c placement and temporary approval as a foster carer under Reg. 25a. Where the local authority is planning to place the child from hospital in an FfA placement, the local authority can prepare the paperwork for the Nominated Officer in advance of the child's birth and initial consideration can be given to this, but the agreement cannot be given till after the child is born so that their specific needs have been considered and the views of the birth mother and other relevant parties have been confirmed.

  Statutory Guidance states clearly that:

  > *Section 22C(9A)-(9C) of the Act does not bring forward the point at which the child is removed from his or her birth parents, or affect the process by which that decision is made. Nor does it affect the process by which the decision to place him or her for adoption is made by the court or affect the rights of the birth family in that regard. If there is no parental consent, the decision whether to authorise the local authority to place the child for adoption remains one for the court at the placement order stage, and the birth parents retain their right to be involved in the process and to have full account taken of their views and wishes, as required.*
  >
  > (DfE, 2015, 3.170)

  The Guidance notes that there are three possible reasons for an FfA placement not leading to adoption: where rehabilitation with the birth family is successful; where suitable family or friends come forward; or where the court does not make a placement order. However, it also states that 'for the vast majority of children who are in a section 22C(9B)(c) placement, progression towards adoption will be the anticipated outcome' (DfE, 2015, 3.147). We would also add a fourth reason, namely where a relinquishing birth parent changes their mind about placing the child for adoption.

FfA under s.20

The duty in s.22C(9)B(c) of the Children Act 1989 to consider placing a child in an FfA placement is the same for all looked after children, whether the child is subject to a care order or looked after under s.20, whenever a local authority is considering adoption for that child.

It should be considered very unusual for an FfA placement to be made when a child is accommodated under s.20, and a placement under such a legal framework should be considered short term only, pending court ratification. Such a placement under s.20 in the short term would allow a child to be placed with his or her potential long-term carers immediately and minimise placement moves for a child who would otherwise have to spend time in a short-term fostering placement. There are three potential situations where it may be appropriate:

- **Child relinquished for adoption:** If a child has been relinquished for adoption, the child will be looked after, and so eligible for an FfA placement, but the appropriate placement within the legal framework would ideally be a placement for adoption with parental consent under s.19 of the Adoption and Children Act 2002. However, if it has not been possible to achieve a matching decision, and so place the child for adoption, it would be possible to approve the intended adopters as foster carers under Reg. 25A of the Care Planning, Placement and Case Review Regulations 2010 and make an FfA placement pending the matching decision.
- **Abandoned child:** Occasionally a parent will be explicit in their intention to relinquish a child for adoption, but fail to engage with Children's Services or CAFCASS to provide the necessary consents. Sometimes a mother (perhaps with significant drug addiction issues) will give birth but leave the child in hospital and lose contact with the child and Children's Services. In such cases, it will be the duty of the local authority to accommodate the child under s.20(1). If family placement options have been ruled out, the child's placement moves could be minimised by placing him or her straight from hospital into an FfA placement. However, the local authority will need to make an immediate application for either a care or placement order (as appropriate) in order to exercise parental responsibility.
- **Placement pending proceedings:** Care proceedings may not be issued pre-birth, so there may occasionally be cases where the local authority has prior knowledge of the family, e.g. knowledge of the parent's previous parenting history, and has already ascertained that there are no suitable family members available to care for the child, and therefore has enough information to consider that the likely outcome for a child is an adoptive placement when the child is born.

  As the local authority is unable to issue proceedings till the child has been born, there will inevitably then be a delay before a court hearing can be achieved. If the threshold for section 3 of the Children Act is met in relation to the child, the local authority should make an urgent application to the court for an interim care order with a hearing on the day or day after the child's birth.
- **Parental consent:** As with any s.20 placement where the birth parents are being asked to consent to accommodation of their child, they must be able to give fully informed consent and know the full details of the

situation to which they are consenting. The President of the Family Division has given clear guidelines, firstly in *R (G) v Nottingham City Council and Nottingham University Hospitals NHS Trust* [2008] EWHC 400 (Admin) and more recently in *Re N* (*Adoption: Jurisdiction*) [2015] EWCA 1112 that should be followed when asking parents to consent to the accommodation of their child. These include: ensuring that the parent has full capacity and understanding of the decision that she is being asked to make; appreciating that she may withdraw her consent at any time, without having to give any reason or notice; and understanding that she retains full parental responsibility and the local authority acquires none.

Although the ruling of Munby P in *Re N* has been qualified in the recent judgement of *London Borough of Hackney v Williams & Anor* [2017] EWCA Civ 26 as being good practice guidance and not an embellishment of the statute, it should nonetheless be followed by a local authority wishing to rely on a parent's consent to a s.20 placement.

Legal advice and information

It might be difficult to be satisfied that a parent has given fully informed consent unless they have had some access to legal advice. Unfortunately, legal aid is not available to fund legal advice for parents considering s.20 accommodation, but it must be axiomatic that where a local authority is considering adoption, they must have concluded that the child is at risk if he or she returns home. It would therefore be appropriate to issue a pre-proceedings letter under the Protocol, even if the intention is, as it must be, to issue proceedings immediately. The letter itself is a passport to some free legal advice that can be provided immediately and allows the parent to give fully informed consent to a s.20 placement if they are satisfied that this would be appropriate.

The parent should also be informed that the local authority's intention is to place the child in an FfA placement and given information, as recommended elsewhere in this guide, about the status of an FfA foster placement and the reasons why the local authority considers that such a placement is appropriate.

Any potential FfA carer being approached to consider an FfA placement of a child under s.20 must be made aware that the parents have the option of removing the child from placement at any time, without giving notice. They would therefore be taking a higher risk than with another FfA placement that the child will not ultimately be placed for adoption with them. There is no additional status conferred on potential adopters/ foster carers by an FfA placement, and the courts will not treat carers who are looking after the child under an FfA placement any differently from other foster carers (*Re T (A Child : Early Permanence Placement)* [2015] EWCA Civ 983).

Points about this to note are:

- There will only be a minority of cases where it is appropriate to make an FfA placement for a child placed under s.20.
- Birth parents must be given full information about the plan to make an FfA placement and enabled to seek appropriate legal advice.
- Prospective FfA carers should be aware of the increased potential for a parent to request the child's return home.
- Where a placement is made under s.20, the local authority must issue their application for a care order as soon as possible and without delay.

Approving FfA carers

The two routes to approving an FfA carer use different legislative frameworks.

- Where an FfA carer is **dual approved**, the prospective adopter must be approved as suitable to adopt under Reg. 30 of the Adoption Agencies Regulations (DfE, 2013b) and also be approved as a foster carer under the Fostering Services Regulations (DfE, 2011). Their approval as a foster carer can include terms of approval being set (Reg. 25 1(b).
- When an FfA placement has become an adoption placement, the FfA carers would usually then want to resign as carers. Their written notice of resignation will lead to their approval being terminated 28 days from the date on which the notice is received by the fostering service provider (DfE, 2011, Reg. 28.13).

Where an FfA carer is given **temporary approval** as a local authority foster carer for the purpose of taking a s.22C placement, the local authority must:

- *be satisfied that placing the child with that particular carer is the most appropriate placement for the child, and that it is in the child's best interests to be placed with them;*
- *have assessed the carer's suitability to care for the child as a foster carer; and*
- *have considered whether placing the child with that carer will safeguard and promote the child's welfare and meet the child's needs as set out in their care plan.*

(DfE, 2010, Reg. 25a (1-2))

Unlike a dual approved carer, an FfA carer who is approved under Reg. 25A does not need to resign as a foster carer. Their temporary approval would automatically expire once the child has been placed for adoption with them under the Adoption Agencies Regulations (DfE, 2015, 3.176). However, the temporary approval can also be terminated by the local authority if a decision is made to remove the child; if their approval as an adopter is terminated; if they are approved as a foster carer under the Fostering Services Regulations; or 28 days after they have given written notice that they no longer wish to be temporarily approved as a foster carer for the child.

Temporary approval as foster carers under Reg. 24 of the Care Planning, Placement and Case Review Regulations 2010

One of the dilemmas for local authorities in making FfA placements for children with adopters of previously adopted siblings has been that these adopters have not necessarily considered or come to the point of reaching a decision to adopt another child. Ideally, the local authority will identify an early need for an FfA placement with a sibling to enable those adopters to consider whether they are able to put themselves forward, initially as FfA carers and then as adopters and to be approved before the placement is needed.

We were made aware of concerns about what information can be shared with prospective carers before the child is born. The advice from CoramBAAF's Legal Consultant is that pre-birth planning will involve some information sharing with potential carers, regardless of whether they are the adopters of a sibling or are mainstream foster carers. Pre-birth, the local authority must be able to discuss a sibling's potential placement without sharing personal information about the birth parents, and to assess the possibilities of placement. In many situations, adopters will be aware of maternal history from their child's placement.

However, there are situations in which timescales do not allow for those adopters to be assessed and approved to take another child. In those cases, some local authorities have been approving the adopters as temporary foster carers under Reg. 24. These regulations require that the local authority decides that the most appropriate placement for the child is with a "connected person", i.e. a relative, friend or person connected with the child; and has assessed their suitability to care for the child, the suitability of their home and all other adults in the household; and is satisfied that the proposed placement will safeguard and promote the child's welfare and meet their needs as set out in the care plan, given the circumstances and taking into account services to be provided (DfE, 2010, Reg. 24(2)). There is currently no precise definition of "connected" in case law or statutory guidance that allows an interpretation categorising the adopter of a sibling as a connected person through the birth connection to their sibling.

Under those regulations, approval will only last for up to 16 weeks while an assessment of the carers as foster carers under the Fostering Services Regulations 2011 (DfE, 2011) is carried out, but can be extended for a further eight weeks (Reg. 25(2)). After that time, either the carers must be approved fully as foster carers or the placement should be terminated, the agency having made other arrangements for the child (Reg. 25.6).

It should be understood that placements made under Reg. 24 where the carers are approved as temporary foster carers but not yet as adopters are *not* recognised as s.22C(9B)(c) placements. The Reg. 24 carers will therefore not be eligible for statutory adoption pay or leave, although some carers in this situation have found that their employer will still make discretionary payments. Agencies should consider subsequently approving these carers as temporary carers under Reg. 25A once they have been approved as adopters, if a placement order is not likely to be made within the 16–24 weeks from their Reg. 24 approval, so they become eligible for this support.

Placement after a placement order has been made

An FfA placement is one that is made *before* the placement order has been made, when the local authority does not have agreement to place the child for adoption.

There are occasionally situations in which local authorities find that they need to place a child with their prospective adopters after the placement order has been made but before the matching panel. In these cases, approved adopters can be given temporary approval under Reg. 25A or be dually approved as foster carers if appropriate assessment has been made of their ability to foster a child. However, the carers would not be entitled to statutory adoption pay and leave from the point of placement, as that entitlement starts only after the matching decision or when a child is placed under Reg. 22A and s.22C(9B) of the Children Act 1989.

Possible situations could include where a child has to make an immediate move from their short-term foster placement before the adoption match can be made and there is an identified need to avoid further placement moves for the child, or where the FfA placement is being made because there has been a challenge from a birth family member to the placement order but there is a desire to prevent a further delay in the child's move to a potential permanent placement. In the latter situation, the prospective carers would need to be made very aware of the potential of the court to make a decision to return the child to a birth parent or family member and the likelihood/probability of them doing so in the specific child's case.

WALES

In Wales, "Fostering to Adopt" was set out in the Social Services and Well-Being (Wales) Act 2014, and Fostering to Adopt placements are made under the Care Planning, Placement and Case Review (Wales)

Regulations 2015. As stated earlier, there are fundamental differences to the model used in England. The following information has been taken from Foster to Adopt Practice Guidance published in 2016 by the National Adoption Service for Wales and AFA Cymru, and is set out for information, whilst recognising that it has limited application for local authorities in England.

In Wales, the duty on local authorities to consider a Foster to Adopt placement is limited to situations where the care proceedings have commenced but the placement order has not been made, and where:

- the agency decision-maker's decision has been made that a child should be placed for adoption; and
- a matching decision under the Adoption Agencies (Wales) Regulations 2005 has been made.

The decision to place will be made by a senior manager – the Nominated Officer, who will have detailed knowledge and understanding of adoption and the role of Foster to Adopt. The guidance suggests that the best placed person to act as Nominated Officer will be the agency decision-maker, as:

> *She or he will have already made the decision that the child should be placed for adoption and will have been the agency decision-maker to decide that the match should be made, following the relevant panel recommendation. She or he may well have been the person to highlight the child's situation as being one which may require a Foster to Adopt placement.*

The prospective adopters will have been approved by a regional collaborative or VAA, and as part of their assessment and preparation they will need to demonstrate:

> *The capacity to manage the fostering task...and abide by the provisions of the Fostering Services (Wales) Regulations 2003. This will include participating in reviews, recording, training and will probably involve facilitating, or at the very least allowing, direct contact with birth family.*

There is a recognised role for the adoption panel noted in the practice Guidance, as follows:

> *The regional collaborative or VAA panel has a role in Foster to Adopt. The panel does not recommend a Foster to Adopt approval, as that is made by the child's local authority's Nominated Officer under Reg. 28. However, a panel cannot ignore the fact that applicants may have stated an interest in Foster to Adopt. Panel will wish to satisfy itself that the applicants are aware of the legal framework for Foster to Adopt, the inherent uncertainties for them and the need to have a different role for the period of the foster placement... If and when appropriate during a matching panel, consideration will need to be given not only to the*

> *match and the requirements of the AA(W)R [Adoption Agencies (Wales) Regulations] 2005 but also to the plan to place the child in a Foster to Adopt placement. Panel will wish to ensure that, again, the prospective adopters and child (if of sufficient age and understanding) understand the legal nature of a Foster to Adopt placement.*

The Practice Guidance recognises that the number of Foster to Adopt placements is likely to be small and notes that:

> *Responsibility for training in respect of the fostering task will remain with the child's local authority, but detailed knowledge of the carer's ability and motivation rests with the regional collaborative or VAA assessor. As the number of Welsh Foster to Adopt placements is likely to be small, it may not be viable for individual local authorities to set up discrete training courses for Foster to Adopt carers. If a match has been made and the prospective adopters have been identified as being interested in Foster to Adopt, it is at this stage that the local authority's family placement team, along with regional collaborative or VAA social worker for the prospective adopters, should ensure that the requisite preparation takes place.*
>
> *There may be a case for local authorities to join together to provide discrete training, support and peer mentoring for this group of carers, jointly co-ordinated with the regional collaboratives, but the child's local authority retains the responsibility, under the CPPCR(W)R [Care Planning, Placement and Case Review (Wales) Regulations] for ensuring that the prospective adopters are fit for the task of fostering on a temporary basis.*

The statutory and regulatory framework for Foster to Adopt in Wales

s.81(10)(11) Social Services and Well-Being (Wales) Act 2014
Adoption Agencies (Wales) Regulations 2005/Reg. 28
Care Planning, Placement and Case Review (Wales) Regulations 2015

Approved prospective adopters (s.81(1)(c)

↓

Child placed with other short-term foster carers at start of care proceedings

↓

Care proceedings

↓

Should be placed for adoption decision (s.81(10)(a)

↓

Matching panel recommendation and agency decision-maker decision (s.81(10)(a)

↓

Carers are temporarily approved as foster carers (Reg. 28)

↓

Child placed with Foster to Adopt carers (as a foster placement)

↓

Care order and placement order made (authority to place)

↓

Foster to Adopt placement becomes adoptive placement

(emphasis added)

Outline of the respective functions of each panel and agency decision-maker

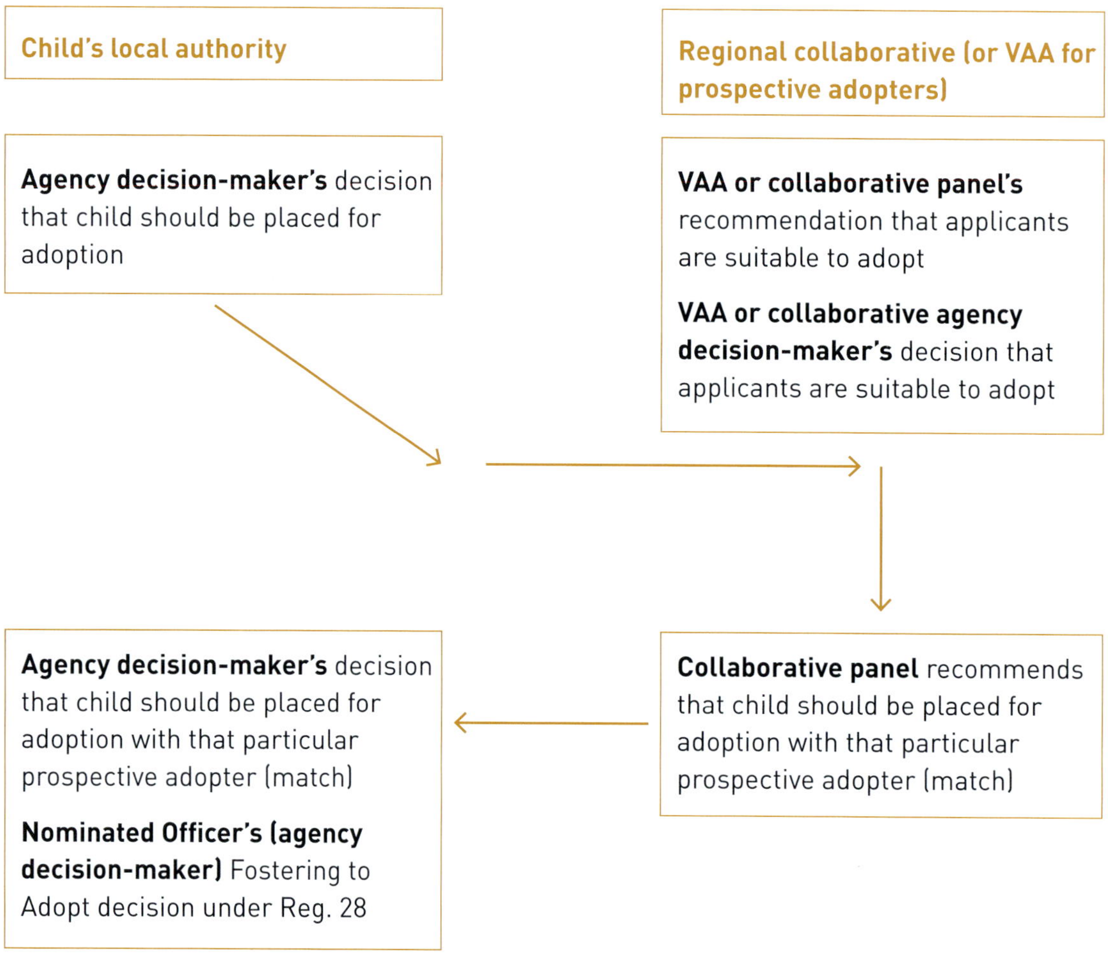

(AFA Cymru, 2016)

Chapter 4
Who are the children?

Guidance and Regulations (DfE, 2015, 1.6) state that:

> *Good social care practice recognises the following principles when working with children and their families:*

- *Time is a crucial element in work with children and should be reckoned in days and months rather than years.*
- *If children have to live apart from their family, both they and their parents should be given adequate information and helped to consider alternatives and contribute to the making of an informed choice about the most appropriate form of care.*

These lead us into considering the children for whom "early permanence" might be appropriate, and then into what the care planning for these children may look like. This chapter focuses on the children who are likely to be placed under FfA.

From recent consultation with adoption agencies and from our questionnaires to FfA adopters, as well as looking back at research into concurrent planning by Coram (2013), it is evident that there are several groups of children for whom early permanence could be achieved through FfA, in the right circumstances. In Coram and BAAF's Practice Guidance on FfA (2013), it is stated that:

> *From the child's perspective, the often lengthy process associated with permanent placement planning and the adoption plan has significant disadvantages. It is well known that the early months and years of a child's life lay the foundation for their development. That foundation is built on the child's need for a stable and loving relational world where they interact with their parents to co-construct a pattern of interactions that ensure that the infant's wide range of needs are met.*

It is noted that:

> *In whatever way these relationship and attachment issues work themselves out during the period of foster care, what is certain is that, where adoption becomes the approved care plan and is endorsed by the court, the relationship with the foster carers and birth parents will be disrupted when the child is finally placed with adoptive parents. For many children that will be the disruption of their relational world formed over months or maybe years. The consequences of this*

disruption are variable and where those involved are well prepared and supported over time, these consequences can be mitigated and new attachment relationships formed, although the challenges should not be underestimated.

However, given all that is known about child development, disrupting attachment relationships is not something that should happen and it is only the force of very difficult circumstances resulting from care planning and the court process that makes this acceptable at all. The current system of balancing the rights and needs of the child and those of the birth parents is fundamental to a humane, fair and just society, but at the heart of that system is a vulnerable child who will carry the longer term consequences of this complex balancing act. Perry (quoted in Borthwick and Donnelly, 2013) comments:

There are critical points during which bonding experiences must be present for the brain systems responsible for attachment to develop normally. These critical periods appear in the first year of life, and are related to the capacity of the infant and the caregiver to develop a positive interactive relationship.

This understanding forms the rationale to place very young babies in the care of families/individuals who will go on to become their lifelong caregivers, thus providing the opportunity for bonding to take place and secure attachment patterns to develop. Such placements avoid the risks associated with multiple caregivers and the child experiencing separations and losses at crucial developmental stages.

In the first instance, it is essential that the local authority has discharged its responsibilities under the Children Act 1989 and the Public Law Outline to consider the viability and appropriateness of birth parents and extended family to care for the child and that these options have been fully explored and evidenced. Where these have been thoroughly examined and ruled out, then FfA may be considered, typically in one of the following circumstances, as identified by Coram and BAAF (2013).

- *Where parents have had one or more children previously placed for adoption or other forms of permanent placement and the evidence strongly suggests that their circumstances have not changed and pose the same risks as they did to previous child/ren. The local authority does not have a proactive plan to rehabilitate the child as the circumstances of the parents are such to pose an ongoing risk.*
- *Where this is the first child, the circumstances of the parents and the risks to the child are such that there is no proactive plan to return the child to the birth parents or to other family members.*
- *Where parents have indicated that they may want their child adopted, but have not formally consented. (s.2(3) Adoption and Children Act 2002)*

There are other circumstances in which placement with a dually approved carer under concurrent planning may be in the interests of the child where there is still exploration of a rehabilitation plan. This would include the capacity to change within the child's timescales.

CIRCUMSTANCES LEADING TO AN FfA PLACEMENT

We now consider the different situations in which a child may be placed with FfA carers.

Where the parents' circumstances are such that the child is deemed to be at risk

> *Factors to be given particular weight in assessing the parenting capacity of the parent include their physical, mental and emotional health and their age. It is known that unless there are adequate protective factors in place, domestic violence, parental alcohol or substance abuse, uncontrolled mental health problems and severe learning difficulties can have an adverse impact on the parent's capacity to safeguard and promote the child's welfare.*
>
> (DfE, 2015, s.3.79)

Where an early assessment of birth family indicates that parents lack the capacity to change their behaviour and that there are no known immediate family members available to care for the child in question, the early permanence options open to the local authority will need to be considered. When considering early permanence, the local authority should also have considered whether there is the potential for viability assessments to be requested for more distant family members so that the possibility of those people putting themselves forward at a later stage to care for the child are minimised once the exploration of identified FfA carers begins.

Where the possibility of further carers coming forward is known, the local authority should advise the potential FfA carers of the identified risks of these leading to the child being moved to an alternative long-term placement. This is a possibility that adoption agencies must make clear when recruiting, preparing and assessing prospective adopters. From the questionnaire results, we learned that in at least one case a child was returned to a member of the extended family who had not been considered as part of initial viability assessments. It is clear that the local authority has a duty to consider all parties put forward to care for the child, and that prospective FfA carers must be prepared for this eventuality.

The Family Rights Group (2014a), in a pamphlet aimed at birth parents, notes:

> *When there are ongoing child protection concerns which have not been sorted out, it is possible that Children's Services might consider it is not safe for your child to remain at home with you. In this situation, Children's Services should work with you and your family to explore all safe options for your child to live with someone else in the family (unless there is an emergency). This means it is really important that you involve members of your wider family as early as possible in helping you make sure your child is safe, whether they stay at home with you or live with someone else in the family. FGCs can be an extremely useful way of doing this. Government guidance says: 'It is important that wider family are identified and involved as early as possible as they can play a key role in supporting the child and help parents address identified problems. Where problems escalate and children cannot remain safely with parents, local authorities should seek to place children with suitable wider family members where it is safe to do so.'*

We would suggest that, in cases where families are previously known to the local authority and there have been previous safeguarding concerns, a Family Group Conference (FGC) as part of pre-birth planning is an essential way of considering all potential carers before the child's arrival. Where the family does not have prior involvement with social care services, but there are concerns about the adults' lifestyles, domestic violence, severe mental ill health and the potential impact of this on the unborn child or on a young child, an FGC might enable the extended family or friendship group to assist, thus avoiding care proceedings.

Robust planning and assessment are required when considering whether a child should not be placed with its birth parents, and where there is a significant chance of the child returning home, it is not appropriate for an FfA placement or concurrent planning to be used. As stated earlier, where the birth family and/or support network have shown a determination to work collaboratively with the local authority, early permanence might not be the best solution. We are firmly of the view that FfA placements should not be used as "emergency" foster placements and that where there is no early assessment of the family and/or connected persons, it becomes more risky to use early permanence as an option. Where a relative or significant person does come forward after the child is placed in FfA, then there should be open and frank discussions with the FfA carers to try and support them through what is likely to be an emotional rollercoaster whilst the viability assessments are carried out.

Placement from hospital

In some situations, a pre-birth conference will have agreed that the parents' circumstances are such that the child is deemed likely to suffer significant harm if placed with the birth parent, that there is no likelihood of parental change, and that any potential family members have been assessed and ruled out. This would then lead to a care plan that the baby is placed, following delivery, with the FfA carers. On occasions, it has been necessary for the baby to spend some time in an intensive care unit (ICU) following delivery, either because of drug withdrawal symptoms or issues associated with prematurity. In these situations, there would be encouragement for birth parents and FfA carers to meet if a risk assessment has been completed prior to this eventuality, due to the likelihood of them meeting on the ward. Where FfA carers are able to have direct contact with the birth parents at an early stage, this will provide insight and experience that can then be shared with their adopted child in the future. Adopters have commented that they have found these early meetings invaluable as they can speak with more authority with their child about how the birth parents appeared and what messages they wanted their child to have. In many ways, it can be comforting for birth parents to meet the potential adopters so that they have something tangible to consider in the future. There is evidence in our questionnaires that supports these views.

> *We had several contact meetings with his birth mother, and one with his birth father too. We had one extra health appointment with a doctor who had known the birth mother and siblings for a long time, plus extra visits from health visitors... We were really glad to meet his birth parents, even though it was very emotional for us and we felt so sad for them.* (CP3)

When a risk assessment has concluded that a meeting between adopters and birth parents is not advisable, it is recommended that the reasons for this are noted in the Child Permanence Report (CPR) and life story work. An example might be where one or both birth parents are particularly violent and hostile and would have the potential to disrupt any meeting. Another situation might involve historical concerns from previous experience where a birth parent has gone on to use information about the adopters on social media. It is important that these reasons are recorded factually so that the adopters and child can have open discussions about this in the future.

Placement from a short-term foster placement

Young children have also been placed for FfA when the birth family history is of such significant concern that extensive plans for assessing the parents are made before the birth of the child in question. The child may be placed from birth with a foster family or, as seen in the example below, the birth mother is placed in a parent and child placement for assessment purposes, but an FfA placement is seen as the next option where the assessment produces a negative outcome:

> *The mother was herself an adopted child who had a troubled history and a history of mental health difficulties. She was placed in an assessment unit with T from T's birth. The assessment was negative and when the placement ended T was placed with FfA carers. Contact continued several times per week until the final hearing. T had been very "shut down" when in her mother's care but her presentation soon changed and when the final hearing approached, the birth parents accepted the plan for adoption and were delighted that T could stay with her carers. T is now adopted.*
>
> (Surrey County Council)

Placement with adopted siblings

Significant numbers of children placed with FfA carers are joining siblings (full or half). The legislation governing the ways in which this is achieved have been covered in the previous section, but it was clear from our discussions with agencies that this is considered for children as part of the care planning process, where:

> *Being able to live with brothers and sisters where they are also looked after is an important protective factor for many looked after children. Positive sibling relationships provide both support in childhood and adulthood and can be particularly valuable during changes in a young person's life... Wherever it is in the best interests of each individual child, siblings should be placed together.*
>
> (DfE, 2015, 3.21–3.23)

Several of the FfA carers we heard from were in this situation and talked about how this prompted their decision to offer FfA.

> *J's older sister had been placed for adoption just prior to his birth. J and his birth mother were in an assessment unit; the assessment was going to be negative and the local authority planned to place J with his siblings under FfA regulations at the end of the proceedings. However, his birth mother abandoned him in the unit which meant that his placement with the FfA carers was unplanned and very sudden. He continued to have contact with his birth parents until the final hearing and the exchanges via the contact book served to develop something of a relationship between adopters and birth parents. The birth parents were delighted that he was placed with his sister and in the end did not contest the plan for adoption at the final hearing.*
>
> (Surrey County Council)

> *We received a letter from the local authority to notify us that the birth parents for our three adopted children were due another baby in eight*

weeks. We were asked if we would consider an FfA placement. Our assigned social worker talked through how the process would work. We were assured that as this baby was their seventh child to go into care, the process should be straightforward. (FfA1)

We hadn't planned to adopt through FfA and had not heard of it. We already had two children and hadn't planned to extend our family further. The local authority contacted us about our third child because we had already adopted a full sibling. We learned about FfA at that point, and wanted to adopt our third child because we strongly believed he should be with his sister. (FfA2)

CASE STUDY: LEEDS CITY COUNCIL

Placing a sibling from hospital using Reg. 24

Child's background information: The birth mother's experiences as a child have been of neglect, abuse and abandonment, and the birth mother described being controlled and physically harmed in her adult relationships, which led to her having significant mental health difficulties and vulnerability. The birth mother has had 11 previous children, all of whom she has been unable to care for. A comprehensive assessment previously completed concluded that she would not be able to safely care for a child and the baby's elder sibling was placed with adoptive parents in 2013. At the time of pregnancy with the new baby, there was no evidence of any changes to the birth mother's lifestyle to enable her to care for a new baby. A further assessment determined that the birth mother and her then partner would not be able to care for the new baby.

Adopters' background information: The early permanence carers are a married couple in their 40s. They are experienced birth parents to two adult children; they have been foster carers to numerous children; and they are now adoptive parents to the baby and her older sister.

How the match was identified: The early permanence carers were the adopters of the baby's maternal half-sibling. They were approached during the pregnancy and given the available information by the local authority, although they were already aware of the maternal history. They were committed to the new baby and approved as kinship carers/connected persons (using a Reg. 24 assessment) prior to her birth. This was to avoid delay and enable the baby to be placed with them whilst they were being assessed as second-time adopters.

Timing of the placement: In order to place the new baby immediately, the early permanence carers were approved as Reg. 24 carers, through their connection to the new baby as the adoptive parents of her older sister. The baby was placed from hospital at five days old.

Supervision and support of placement and any issues such as contact: The early permanence carers are committed to contact and had forged a relationship with the birth mother when facilitating contact with the baby's elder sibling as foster carers, and they were happy to undertake this with the new baby. However, contact had to be arranged for when their older child attended nursery, as she no longer had contact, being in an adoptive placement.

Outcome: Once the legal process had been completed and a placement order obtained, the carers applied immediately for an adoption order, which was granted with no contest.

Relinquished babies

In addition to the use of FfA placements for children going through care proceedings, we have identified that agencies are using early permanence placements when children are relinquished by their birth parent/s. The case examples we heard about suggest that many of these situations are not straightforward, as can be seen in the following example that shows how an agency managed an extremely complex case of relinquishment.

CASE STUDY: DONCASTER CHILDREN'S SERVICES TRUST

Placing a relinquished baby

The adoption team was informed that a birth mother had attended the Pregnancy Advisory Service, and being estimated at 28 weeks and five days pregnant, she was too far into the pregnancy for a termination. Information was received that this may be a potential FfA placement for an unborn child as she was indicating that she wished to relinquish the baby. The birth mother engaged minimally during the pregnancy so that there were limited opportunities to share information about her family history. The birth mother and her siblings were not known to social care and there were no records available to gather further information.

The birth mother was a 17-year-old child from an Irish Travelling background, and to protect herself from the community, she shared little information and her engagement with social care and health professionals was minimal.

Some information was shared about her and her extended family's health and any genetic conditions for the purposes of medical information. The birth mother explained that her extended family were all in good health and did not have any disability or genetic conditions. She also explained that she was educated in mainstream school up until the age of 11 years and then was given personal tuition until the age of 15 years.

It was evident that the birth mother felt unable to confide in anyone in her social group. She not only feared for her own safety and well-being, but also that of others. She was protective of others by deliberately not informing anyone of her situation, and due to her feeling about risks to herself, she had been unable to entrust anyone in her network with her decision to relinquish her baby.

During the latter stages of the pregnancy, a prospective adoptive family had been approached to consider offering an FfA placement to the relinquished baby. They were given all available information and accepted the risks. They accepted that there was no information on the health and genetic history of the birth father and extremely limited information on the birth mother and the maternal extended family. They also understood that during the six weeks following the child's birth, the birth mother might change her mind and request the return of the child. They were offered significant support by their adoption social worker and were made aware of the agency requirements of foster carers taking baby placements.

Following the birth, the female baby was deemed to be healthy and the birth mother refused to have any contact with her. The baby was placed with the FfA carers who had been approached in the weeks leading up to the birth and who came to the hospital to collect the child. In this case, the birth mother did not want to meet them.

The birth mother made no attempts to see her child and became quite elusive after the birth. The social worker contacted her by text to advise her that she needed to sign various papers, and she did meet CAFCASS workers – she knew that if she didn't, this would lead to court proceedings that could create further complications for her.

Issues to consider

During our discussions with agencies, it became clear that FfA is being used for "relinquished" babies in the six-week period before formal consent has been given.

Whilst the advantages for the child and the carers are clear where the child is being placed from birth, it is important that FfA carers are very clear about the status of these placements in the first six-week period and prior to the formal consent being witnessed by CAFCASS, and the option for birth mothers/parents to change their minds. We were made aware of a case in which birth parents had requested the return of their child when the baby was 10 weeks old.

In some cases where the care plan has been made with birth parents prior to the baby's birth, the FfA carer has been at the hospital. In some cases, the birth mother has met the adopters at this stage but this has not always been the case. In the case study above about a relinquished baby, the birth mother was disengaged with the process and had no intention of seeing her baby, let alone meeting the prospective adopters. The social worker and health professionals worked extremely hard to try and obtain as much information as they could from her about her family background, family health and anything else that might assist the adopters in parenting the child effectively throughout life. The worker was determined to provide as much information as possible so that the child in later life had some sense of where she came from. In this case, the birth mother's cultural background was a factor in the relinquishment and needed explanation from the birth mother so that it could then be explored throughout the child's life.

In other examples we have been given, birth parents did meet the FfA carers and, although difficult at the time, the adoptive families expressed the view that, as their child grows up, it will be of benefit to be able to say that they met his or her birth relatives.

> *Because we have met her birth parents and got to know them a little bit, it means that we can always tell her about them as she is growing up, how much they wanted to keep her and what kind of people they are. We think this will be important for her.*
>
> (Early permanence carer quoted in Early Permanence Resource Pack, Leeds City Council, 2015)

> *We met with the birth mother. It was a massively positive experience for everyone involved and the birth mother told us that she was happy for us to call our son "our son". While we don't feel we needed to hear this for our own sake, we feel that it will be a very strong and important message for him when we explain his story.* (FfA3)

It should be noted that whilst using FfA for relinquished babies, Adoption Statutory Guidance 2013, 2.48–2.52 does set out a process for managing the placement of relinquished babies, and local authorities should consider whether this would be a more appropriate way of achieving the best outcome for the child.

Older children

Although the majority of children considered for FfA are under two years old, there are examples of local authorities using FfA for older children or sibling groups where initial care proceedings have identified that they cannot return safely to members of the birth family or extended network. This would normally be where long-term social care intervention and support have been unable to alter patterns of adult behaviour that pose a risk to the child. In discussions with Devon County Council regarding early permanence, it was noted that although initially used mainly for children under 12 months, the council has now extended the consideration and use of FfA to all children being placed for adoption, where appropriate, including older children and sibling groups, so that about 65 per cent of children being adopted in Devon now are placed initially in an FfA placement. This includes a small number who are placed after the placement order has been made due to the individual circumstances of the case.

When considering the use of FfA for older children, thought must be given to issues such as placement security: if the child is still having contact with extended family members, how safe will their placement be if it becomes an adoptive placement? The verbal child is very likely to talk to the birth family members about where they are living, the nursery or schools they are attending and activities that they are engaged in. Where there are deemed to be few risks associated with birth families, this may be appropriate. However, children should never be made to feel that they have to "keep secrets", and thought must be given prior to placement about how confidentiality will be maintained. This should form part of the early assessment work and be discussed in detail with any prospective adopters interested in offering FfA.

The child will need to be prepared for the placement and it is important to consider what explanation will be given to them as part of their preparation. This explanation will need to be consistent with that given to birth family members to avoid any mixed messages being given to the child, for example, will they be aware that this is a placement where they can stay through to adulthood if they cannot return to their birth family? They should not be placed in a situation where they may experience divided loyalties between their FfA carers and birth parents.

Another issue to be discussed and agreed will be what the child will call his or her new family. We would suggest that the usual expectation would be that children are encouraged to call the FfA carers by their first names, with a view to gradually changing to "Mum or Mummy" and "Dad or Daddy" only after the placement has been recognised as an adoption placement and the child has become more settled and secure. The point at which this change happens would need to go at the child's pace. This is an area that will need further discussion with the extended family of the FfA carers to ensure a consistent approach.

Where siblings are being considered for an FfA placement, it would be expected that a full sibling assessment would have formed part of the pre-proceedings work. These placements should not therefore be seen in the same way as "emergency" foster placements. Where little is known or where there are significant concerns about sibling relationships, it is not appropriate for FfA placements to be used.

Some examples of placing older children are noted below.

CASE STUDY: GLOUCESTERSHIRE COUNTY COUNCIL

Placing older children

A five-year-old boy (B) had recently become subject to a placement order. He was self-harming, and was re-traumatising himself and his sisters, often on a daily basis. After several placement moves, an FfA placement was sought. An approved adopter, who had the skills and personality to cope with B's behaviours, was identified. Reg. 25A was used to approve the adopter as an FfA carer for B. B needed a lot of nurturing and patience – he was scared, found simple tasks like getting in the car difficult, and needed his carer to understand the reasons behind his behaviour, help him to name his emotions and reassure him that she was there for him. Contact with his siblings continued, fully supported by his carer.

B was matched and later adopted by his FfA carer. She had developed a good relationship with his sisters, which will help with ongoing future contact. His sisters too have been placed for adoption and contact features in all their plans and is fully supported by the adopters.

B continues to need support through Children and Young People Services and he has made remarkable progress in all aspects of his life. He has a positive attachment to his adoptive mother and he is happy. He has been able to talk to his mother about things that happened to him when he lived with his birth parents and life story work has been completed with him.

During discussions in our focus groups, we were advised of some cases where FfA placements had been used following the adoption disruption of slightly older children with complex needs. One situation described where a four-year-old girl had been placed with a family and that, some weeks after placement, the adopters had decided that this was not the right child for their family. To avoid too many moves, another adoptive family was sought and identified and the child then moved to these adopters, initially on a fostering basis. This allowed the child to become accustomed to the new family and to manage some of her confusion and sadness at leaving her first adoptive family. The FfA carers recognised that the child needed some time to settle and they too felt it was right that she should not be overwhelmed by being told that they were her "new" adopters.

This is an example of a situation where dually approved carers were used for a child already subject to a placement order but where the individual circumstances of the case led to social workers deciding that the use of FfA carers was appropriate. As stated previously, an FfA placement when a placement order is already in place, does not attract statutory adoption pay and leave, and local authorities would need to be very clear with the FfA carers about how this would be financially supported.

Placement from home

It would be more unusual to consider placing a child in an FfA placement when they were being placed from home. Much would depend on the assessed strengths of the prospective carers to manage the additional unknowns and uncertainties. However, we were told of some such placements and an example is provided below.

CASE STUDY: SHEFFIELD CITY COUNCIL

Placement from home

A couple were assessed and approved by the local authority and keen to take an early permanence placement/sibling group. The male applicant had experience of fostering in his extended family and the female applicant had experience of working with young children. They were approved in 2016 and a sibling pair was placed with them soon after.

The brother and sister were born in 2012 and 2015 respectively. There had been a long history of social care involvement with the birth family and issues of domestic violence and significant child neglect were evident. There was significant concern about the children and care proceedings were initiated. The adoption team heard of the imminent removal of the children from their birth parents and felt that there might be a possible match with the approved adopters. The adoption worker explored the possibility of this potential link as an early permanence placement/FfA situation with management and the field work team, and all felt that it had potential. A rigorous support package was put in place involving meetings with the MAPS (multi-agency psychological service) team, weekly visits, and a foster carer mentor. But in effect, the FfA carers proved to be excellent in understanding the children's needs. This was possibly supported by some knowledge of looked after children in the female carer's family as her mother had worked with them in schools, and the male carer had grown up alongside foster children as his aunt had been a foster carer. There are also adopters within their extended family.

During the early stages of the placement, the boy exhibited a number of challenging behaviours that required a very firm approach by both carers. The children were having contact with their birth parents and the FfA carers transported them. On one occasion, the carers met one of the parents and, although difficult, it was managed well.

The link was approved at the panel after the care order and placement order were made. The panel advised that significant support packages should be made available as and when required, given the level of trauma experienced by the children.

The placement is going very well. Since the initial stages of placement, the family has not required additional support.

It is important to consider that although the benefit of a placement from home is likely to be less stressful for children as they will only experience one move – from their birth family to the new prospective FfA carer – there will be additional risks to this type of placement that should be carefully considered:

- There may have been limited opportunities to assess the child and their physical, developmental and emotional needs, particularly if the child is not seen regularly outside of the family situation.
- The child's understanding of why he or she is being moved might be very limited and there may have been minimal opportunity of eliciting his or her wishes and feelings.
- If there is limited information about the birth family dynamics and the child's experiences in the family home, then the FfA carers may inadvertently employ parenting strategies that cause stress reactions in the child.
- There may not have been an opportunity to undertake an informed sibling assessment to inform decisions about placing a sibling. The need for these assessments, which are key in informing planning for siblings, is highlighted by the issues raised by Burnell *et al* (2009):

> *In contemporary literature there is still a view that, on balance, placing siblings together is a good thing for placement stability and for child development. Rushton* et al *(2001) found that children who had been rejected by birth parents had a better outcome when placed with their siblings. For the child there is continuity, security and an affirmation of identity. However, on the converse, other recent research has shown that disruption is more likely to follow when a child is violent or sexually abusive to other children and siblings (Lowe and Murch* et al*, 1999). In a study of sexually abused children it was found that, where there were high levels of sexual acting out between siblings, this led to placement breakdowns (Farmer and Pollock, 1998). Behavioural problems and conflictual relationships with carers and adoptive parents are highly correlated with destabilising placements.*

In situations where the local authority is considering the possibility that a child may be placed directly from the birth family, it is essential that a full family assessment has taken place and that the child's lived experiences can be explored with the FfA carers prior to placement. The prospective adopters must be prepared for the likelihood of "triggers" occurring and should be given clear guidance on how to manage unusual or unexpected behaviours. This is where links to other foster carers and adopters who have been through similar experiences will be invaluable. Until the child actually moves into the FfA placement, it is unlikely that the full extent of their home life experiences will be known and part of the uncertainty of taking older children will be how trauma manifests itself. It is therefore most important that the prospective adopters are open to whatever support is deemed necessary to help the child settle and the family to bond. If it is known that the child has been subjected to a range of abusive behaviours, it may not be a good plan to consider early permanence through FfA.

CHECKLIST FOR PRACTITIONERS

- Be clear that all family members have been explored during pre-proceedings work.
- Where a child is to be relinquished, ensure that all practitioners, including health professionals involved, understand the concept and process for FfA and are working to the same guidelines.
- Consider whether there is a need for DNA testing to confirm or rule out paternity prior to an FfA placement being made.
- Ensure that birth parents have access to accurate and appropriate information about FfA that is understood by them.
- Where siblings are to be considered for early permanence, ensure that a sibling assessment is carried out prior to making an FfA placement.
- Where a child is being placed with adopted siblings, consider the impact on the siblings as well as the prospective carers if the child was to return to their birth family.
- Consider how an older child should be prepared for an FfA placement and how to manage the additional issues about confidentiality and divided loyalties.
- Ensure that FfA is considered for all children subject to a plan for adoption, including older children and siblings where appropriate.
- Where it is an older child being placed, consideration would also need to be given to how this would be managed if a return home was then the outcome.

Chapter 5
Care planning and placement

In this chapter, we focus on care planning for the placement – the actions of the local authority, routes by which a child may be placed, the position of birth parents, and the position of FfA carers.

ACTIONS OF THE LOCAL AUTHORITY

FfA may be considered at various points along the care planning continuum and *must* be considered when the local authority is considering adoption as set out in s.22C(9B)(c) of the Children Act 1989. It should involve representatives from all the relevant teams in children's services. Local authorities should ensure that health professionals and CAFCASS are aware of and understand the rationale for early permanence. In order to achieve seamless practice for children with a potential care plan of adoption, it is necessary for all agencies to have clear structures in place that all practitioners, managers and independent reviewing officers (IROs) understand and work to.

> *A placement made following consideration under s.22C(9B)(c) of the Act (an s.22C(9B)(c) placement) with carers who are both approved adopters and approved foster carers is a fostering placement under the Act and one which may lead to adoption by those foster carers. The advantage of this type of placement is that the child will be placed with foster carers who, subject to a placement order being made, or parental consent, are expected to go on to become the child's adoptive family. Delay in finding a permanent family for young children who have already experienced neglect early on in their lives may have a profoundly damaging effect on their development. This type of placement has potential to reduce this delay and the damage caused significantly.*
>
> (DfE, 2015, s.3.145)

Statutory Guidance and the Children Act 1989 (s.22C(9B)(c)) make clear that for every child who may have an adoption plan, consideration must be given to placing that child in a placement with approved adopters who are also approved foster carers. This should be included in legal planning meetings, permanency planning meetings, adoption tracking meetings, reviews and any other professional meetings about the child. It is therefore most important that agency protocols reflect this and that they are inclusive and available to all professionals working with the child and his or her birth family, and that adoption team managers or staff are included in these meetings.

TOOLS TO AID DECISION MAKING

Through our focus groups and contact with agencies, we have been provided with a range of the materials that agencies are currently using to promote and support the use of FfA; some examples of these are included in the Appendices.

Gloucestershire County Council, for instance, provides social workers with a Screening Matrix (Appendix 2) that looks at criteria to be assessed alongside the assessment of the birth family. This guides the child care social worker to consider whether or not issues such as domestic violence or substance misuse have been features in the child's lived experience and whether or not there have been deficits in parenting this child and/or others. The Matrix is designed to enable all workers to start thinking about the possibility of the use of an early permanence placement at a very early stage of the likelihood of this child requiring permanence away from their birth parents and extended family. Gloucestershire County Council then provides an Early Permanence Placement Referral Form for workers to complete (see Appendix 3), that considers significant issues such as location of birth family, potential issues for the child and what skills the prospective FfA carer might have to offer.

Some agencies have developed various tools/paperwork to track and plan for children in their care, including specific flowcharts to enable practitioners to see clearly how and where early permanence planning and FfA fit into the wider care planning process in their authority. One example of such a flowchart has been devised by Essex County Council Adoption Service and shared across workers in their children's services (see below). It clearly shows who is responsible for each stage in the process when the FfA placement leads to an adoption order being made. We would suggest when developing a flowchart that it should also show the pathway where the child returns to their birth parents or extended family member.

Early permanence pathway

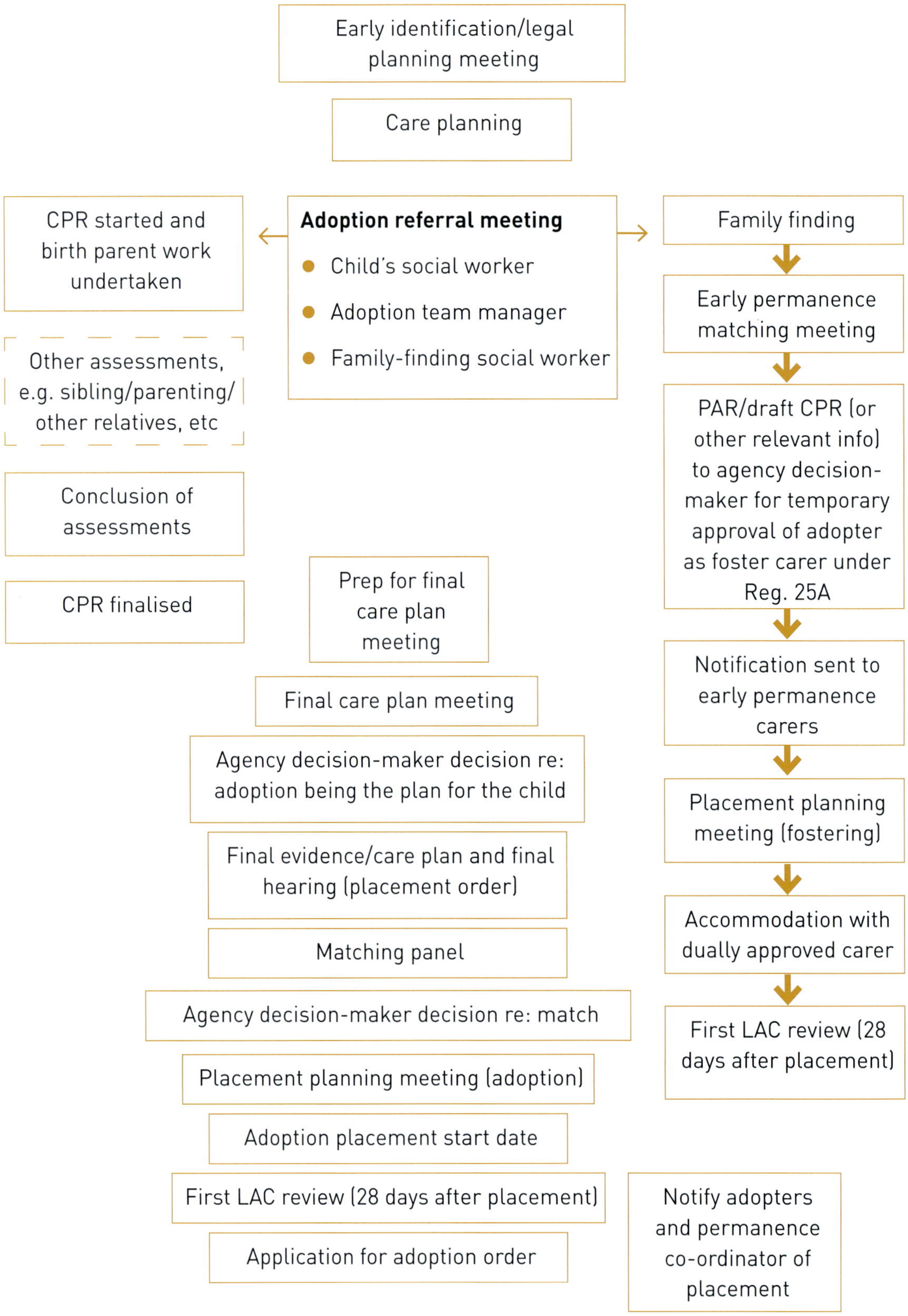

(Reproduced with permission from Essex County Council, 2016)

THE DECISION-MAKING PROCESS

Appendix 4 includes a comprehensive Checklist for Social Workers from Northamptonshire County Council that is particularly helpful in identifying all relevant aspects in the care plan, in what sequence they should be considered, and who should undertake which tasks. This checklist is a good example of how a policy document can draw workers' attention to the importance of pre-birth planning and pre-proceedings work. It asks key questions about, for example, whether a Family Group Conference has been held, whether potential family members and friends have been considered and ruled out, and whether there are any issues about paternity. The checklist requires workers to comment on all these issues and to give dates when information was received and decisions made. It is an example of clear case planning and takes the worker through each different stage of the process of achieving an FfA or concurrent planning placement.

Whilst the responsibility for decision making lies with the local authority, it will need to co-ordinate and seek the involvement and contributions of others, including health and other professionals involved in working with the birth parents (police, drug and alcohol services, mental health workers, asylum-seeking teams, etc).

Where it is identified that a plan of adoption is one of the outcomes being considered, it is most important that the children's social work teams involve the family-finding and adoption services at an early stage. This may be an in-house adoption team, an adoption consortium that will include VAAs as well as local authority adoption services, or a regional adoption agency (RAA). This early involvement ensures that the family placement services can contribute their specialist knowledge to the decision-making process and gives them more time to consider whether there are "in-house" prospective adopters who might be appropriate if an FfA placement is needed, or whether enquiries need to be made outside the agency's resources.

Rotherham Metropolitan Borough Council advised us that they have developed a robust early identification process that involves legal services, child care teams and the adoption service. They have developed efficient systems and open communication so that unborn children at risk and likely to need early permanence are identified early on and work is then completed prior to care proceedings to consider the viability of extended family, etc.

IDENTIFYING AN APPROPRIATE FfA PLACEMENT

CCS Adoption has a Fostering for Adoption Placement Protocol that identifies several tasks that should be completed by the local authority prior to the final decision to implement an FfA plan. This suggests that any child with a plan for FfA should have a genogram showing all family members, an up-to-date chronology and DNA test results (if relevant). It also identifies that for young children, a risk assessment should be completed to consider the child's current and predicted needs, the birth family circumstances (including health and any other identified issues, social presentation, location, etc). This will inform decision making about an appropriate match to an FfA carer.

There may be cases where it is identified that a child should be placed in an FfA placement out of area, perhaps through a consortia arrangement or a VAA, because specific skills or experience are being sought in a suitable prospective adopter, or perhaps because it is deemed too "risky" for the child to remain in his or her original location. Consideration will also need to be given to how such a placement might impact on the child, and if longer journey times to contact meetings result in additional stresses for the child and greater disruption to their daily routines. In such a case, practitioners might need to consider whether such an FfA placement is the right option for this child.

ENSURING THAT THE PLACEMENT MEETS THE CHILD'S NEEDS

Thought must be given as to how the FfA placement will meet the requirements of the wider care plan whilst the child is looked after. This includes **health needs**: for example, whether this FfA placement can meet the child's health needs, as set out in statutory guidance (DfE, 2015, 2.54).

- *routine checks of the child's general state of health, including dental health;*
- *treatment and monitoring for identified health or dental care needs;*
- *preventative measures such as inoculation;*
- *screening for defects of vision or hearing;*
- *advice and guidance on promoting health and effective personal care;*
- *planned changes to current arrangements.*

Where a child is to be placed in an FfA placement out of area, the placing local authority must notify the clinical commissioning group (CCG) in the area in which the child is to be placed.

> *An informed and sensitive approach is especially necessary for these children since they will often have suffered early disadvantage and may be at risk of their health being compromised because they have not received continuity of care.*
>
> (DfE, 2015, 2.63)

Some FfA adopters we spoke to commented on the problems of health professionals not really understanding the concept of early permanence, the role and responsibility of the FfA carer, and the importance of confidentiality, and described the frustration they experienced when taking the baby/child to routine appointments as well as for more complex medical interventions. This leads us to suggest that agency protocols must include information for all health professionals who may come into contact with these placements. For example, Being Family, the Yorkshire and Humber Adoption Consortium, has produced a brochure specifically for health professionals (an Early Permanence Project Resource Pack (Leeds City Council, 2015)) that offers helpful guidance on pre-birth planning, the perinatal period and post-placement. This is used by all the agencies in the consortium, and has been shared with us by Leeds City Council (see Appendix 5).

Other local authorities have produced similar guidance and it is evident that, where there are robust regional health groups in operation, early permanence remains high on the agenda for discussion and development.

Educational needs form part of the child's care plan and where a child is of nursery or school age, then the FfA carer must be assessed as suitable to 'ensure that a looked after child of whatever age has the opportunities to achieve educational outcomes comparable to his/her peers' (DfE, 2015, 2.68).

In the case of older children in FfA placements, it is important that appropriate educational professionals are advised of the concept of early permanence and how delegated authority is managed during the fostering phase. It would be good practice to involve Virtual Heads and designated teachers in training and development work relating to early permanence so that the child's lived experience in school or nursery is as uncomplicated as possible. Adoption UK and PAC-UK have produced resources that relate to adopted children in education, and although not specifically geared to FfA, there are many useful topics that can assist teaching staff in becoming more aware of the needs of the children in their classrooms (see www.adoptionuk.org/resources/education-resources and www.pac-uk.org/education).

CONTACT ARRANGEMENTS

Within the care plan, the local authority also has a duty to consider contact arrangements for the child. The role and experience of FfA carers in relation to contact arrangements are covered more fully in Chapter 7, but good planning of contact arrangements is key to the child's well-being, the experiences of both the birth parents and FfA carers, and the selection of the placement.

Borthwick and Donnelly (2014) set out the areas for consideration when planning contact in concurrent planning and we have adapted these where needed to take account of the differing nature of an FfA arrangement. In an FfA placement where the local authority is not actively assessing or planning rehabilitation, the primary purpose of contact is likely to be to enable the birth parents or other family members to retain a relationship with the child while longer-term decisions are made. The frequency of contact should therefore meet the agreed purpose and robust representations should be made to the court where planned contact is not felt to be in the child's best interests. However, as stated previously, arrangements may have to change in response to further assessments being ordered by the court. The key points, adapted from Borthwick and Donnelly (2014, pp109–115), are highlighted below.

Contact agreements

The key contact arrangements will be agreed in court. A working contact agreement should then be drawn up and agreed by all parties. The agreement should set out detailed expectations and ground rules. For example, it should explain who is allowed to attend contact, the timings, the taking of photos, and situations in which contact will not take place, e.g. should the parent arrive under the influence of drugs or alcohol. It should be made clear that any workers assessing the birth parents, and the Children's Guardian, may also attend sessions as part of their work and that the birth parents will be informed beforehand about such arrangements. The review of contact arrangements and the timescale for this must also be agreed, particularly if birth parents do not adhere to the agreement, or family members fail to notify the agency when they cannot attend.

The infant or very young child's needs and circumstances

At the heart of the plan must be consideration of the infant's needs for a secure attachment and predictable routines. Contact cannot replicate the experience of 24-hour care by highly attuned and sensitive carers who are providing a secure base for the child. Contact has the potential to disrupt this secure base and will need to be carefully managed by birth parents, carers and supervisors.

Settling-in time

When the placement plan is agreed, the infant or very young child will move to their carer either from their birth parents or family, hospital or from another foster carer. For some children, this separation will result in mourning the loss of previous carers. In addition, some children will have suffered abuse or neglect and a range of other adverse experiences. Research and good practice indicate that they will need a period of time, at least a few days, to settle into their new placement with their carers without undue disturbance before the first contact visit is arranged and takes place or is restarted.

The individual needs of the birth parents and other family members

For contact to be meaningful and work well, it is very important that the needs and circumstances of the parents and birth family have been fully assessed. Birth parents will be facing a number of major challenges due to the issues that have prevented them from being suitable parents to their child, including alcohol and/or drug misuse, mental illness, learning difficulties and domestic violence. There may also be other impairments that impact on their daily functioning. Any of these may result in a range of vulnerabilities and this will include many feelings about their child being removed from their care and the possibility of this being permanent. There may also be particular needs arising from their cultural background and language that must be taken into account.

Within all of these considerations, birth parents will need to be helped to plan their travel arrangements to and from contact. They will need to be supported to think through what they can realistically expect from contact and what they might feel about their child and meeting their child's carers. They will need to think about who they can turn to in managing their emotions at times when the infant shows a clear preference for the (FfA) carer if they are present at any point of the contact. This is where a dedicated contact supervisor can help.

The involvement of FfA carers

Where possible, local authorities felt it was important that FfA carers were involved in providing the transport to and from contact for the child, but this will need to be subject to an exploration of any assessed risk to their or the child's safety, for example, if a parent or relative has threatened violence or shown a determination to find the carer's address. Where there is a significant risk identified, it may not be appropriate to use an FfA placement. Consideration will need to be given to how they will travel and over what distance, bearing in mind the needs of infants and very young children. Good practice and the experience of the English (concurrent planning) projects suggest that a 20-mile radius is usually realistic, but the actual travel time will need careful consideration. Carers may also need to be available to return to the contact centre early should the infant require this, and their views on this should be sought.

If they do transport the child, the FfA carers will also need to consider what they will do whilst the contact visit is taking place. It can be particularly painful for carers when/if they hear the infant's distress when being left for contact. Their care will be scrutinised by the birth parents and they may feel personally criticised. Opportunities to debrief and be supported will be needed.

Consideration should be given to the arrangements at the start and end of contact, for example, whether birth parents are asked to arrive first, and then carers to leave first at the end of contact to avoid meeting.

Handovers of the infant or very young child at contact

Where the FfA carers are asked to undertake handovers with the birth parents at the contact venue, they need to be prepared for what can be an emotionally stressful event for all parties. Recognising the emotional impact of the physical handover, one agency reported that they ask carers to bring the child in a car seat or pram rather than physically handing over the baby, and ask birth parents to do the same at the end handover.

FfA carers may be asked to exchange information with the birth parents about the progress of the child and convey this in a sensitive way, possibly through a diary or contact book. In some instances, the birth parents may also want to contribute to the diary/contact book, commenting on what has taken place during contact. These exchanges can be an important component of life story material for the child, but caution will be needed to ensure that there is no identifying information given in the contact book.

The frequency and length of contact

As already stated, each contact plan should be tailored to each infant's needs, and research and practice experience should inform this. There should be close liaison between the child's social worker, the carer's social worker and the local authority lawyer in considering the most appropriate plan and making representations to the court, where needed. Contact sessions should be held at the same times and on the same days, wherever possible; this may need to change in line with the child's changing developmental needs and progress of the plan. The emphasis must be on the quality of contact from the child's perspective.

Venue

The venue for contact is very important, and it needs to be a safe, accessible and familiar environment with a welcoming and comfortable atmosphere and an appropriate range of facilities, including age-appropriate toys. There should be facilities for preparing and heating food and making bottles as required, along with facilities for changing and bathing the child. Workers need to be available to greet people as they arrive. The contact supervisor (ideally someone who is known to both the carers and birth parents) should be on site to facilitate the handovers of the child and be present during the session itself.

Where FfA carers are attending the venue, the workers present and the carers should be aware of the importance of maintaining confidentiality, for example, signing-in books should only require their first names, and no details of car registration should be shared.

Transportation

If a decision is taken that it is not appropriate/possible for the FfA carer to be involved in transporting the child, then an escort, preferably the contact supervisor, will need to be arranged. This person should be introduced to the child beforehand and should remain a consistent escort throughout travel arrangements to support the child during the journeys and reassure the carers.

Contact supervision

The role and function of the contact supervisor is fundamental to contact working most effectively. Continuity and consistency of supervisor are key components and it is important that the supervisor's involvement in contact is an active one. They are there to maintain safety and observe interactions, but also to facilitate a good experience for the child and to support the birth parents to improve their skills. Contact supervisors therefore need the skills, knowledge and authority to undertake this important task. Regular reviews should be held where there are ongoing concerns about the quality of the contact experience.

There may not be time for full feedback to the carers at the end of contact and the supervising social worker should have oversight of the carers' experience of contact and ensure that they have the opportunity to receive and give feedback about the experience for the baby. It may be helpful for the contact supervisor to visit the carers and baby at home to observe the baby in the care environment so that they can comment on any differences noted during contact visits.

However, caution is needed in feedback given to FfA carers about any aspects of assessment of the birth parents and how they present in contact, as this is confidential information. It can also be difficult for the carers if they are given too much information about the birth parents, as issues can change from day to day.

Recording and reports about contact

The contact supervisor will need to make notes during the contact sessions as appropriate and prepare regular reports on these sessions.

The contact agreement should detail how contact will be recorded and how birth parents will be provided with access to these reports.

(The above material has been adapted from Borthwick and Donnelly, 2013, pp 109–115.)

In the materials devised by agencies, we have noted that, in their early permanence protocols, every effort has been made to ensure that the issue of contact is thoroughly explored. Essex County Council, for example, has a section in their procedures for early permanence that clearly identifies what contact arrangements will need to be managed, including frequency, supervision of contact, risks and strengths, contact book, expectations of birth parents, expectations of FfA carers, etc (see Appendix 6).

BARRIERS TO CONSIDERING EARLY PERMANENCE

It has been reported that in some organisations early permanence has been viewed with some suspicion and there have been concerns expressed by workers that these placements pre-empt a court decision. In our focus groups and discussions with agencies, we found that certain barriers to considering such placements are evident.

- The "culture" of the organisation appears to be an issue. For example, in some areas where the responsibility for developing early permanence is held exclusively by one team (e.g. the adoption team), there is a danger that other parts of the child care service may feel or be excluded from that development and that the seamless care planning required does not happen. Alternatively, we have noted that, in agencies with good communication between referral and response teams, the child protection services, including legal teams, reviewing officers, fostering and adoption teams and CAFCASS, then more successful early permanence planning has taken place and more placements have been made.
- Where agencies have identified a "champion" for early permanence, they have been shown to have broken down the barriers to successful early permanence placements.
- Where the agency has a clear process for early permanence referrals that is supported by fostering and adoption teams as well as the rest of the child care service, FfA is managed more effectively. In Cambridge City Council, for example, the family-finding team takes responsibility to review the child's profile after initial identification and to explore permanence options. A summary is then provided to the agency decision-maker advising why an FfA placement should be agreed in the care plan. The medical adviser then pieces together a robust health profile for the FfA carers for this child to raise awareness of potential

health uncertainties and potential learning difficulties, etc. This is a clear process and all practitioners are aware of the agency protocol. In other agencies, permanence teams may take on this role.

We believe the evidence shows that it is essential to have someone within the agency dedicated to considering early permanence placements, and recognise that this will require further consideration and planning in the development of RAAs. This will need to include senior management endorsement, but for day-to-day purposes could be invested in a practitioner or team manager lead person.

Rotherham Metropolitan Borough Council, for example, has an early permanence "champion" who is a practitioner in the adoption service. Her role is to work closely with all other colleagues in the child care service and to ensure that early permanence is considered for all children who may have a care plan of adoption. Over the last two years, Rotherham has developed its early permanence planning practice in conjunction with its legal and child care locality teams. The champion, in conjunction with adoption team managers, works with cases where a potential early permanence placement has been identified. Legal planning meetings for unborn children always consider whether early permanence might be appropriate and all teams are aware of the procedures for this. The champion does much of the exploration of the child's background information and will then liaise with colleagues in the locality and in adoption to look for potential FfA placements. She also provides training for colleagues and prospective adopters and feels strongly that their practice reflects the hard work that has gone into developing it.

In other agencies, such as Devon County Council, the development and implementation of early permanence has been very much driven by senior managers in both adoption and care services. There is a monthly permanency tracking panel that looks at all children in care from their first month in care. The panel includes an area manager, legal representative, fostering manager, adoption manager and a manager from the intervention services. The panel ensures that early permanence is being considered as part of permanence planning for children.

There is evidently not a "national approach" to the planning and delivery of early permanence at this stage and agencies appear to have developed an approach that fits with their wider service configuration.

In agencies where there is ongoing uncertainty about roles and responsibilities of those involved in early permanence, the numbers of FfA placements are lower. For example, where the agency does not have clear publicity and information for prospective adopters about the "practicalities" of FfA, then a limited number of prospective adopters are likely to consider it. Where agencies have developed robust information packs (hard copy and/or online) and they have clarity about what is expected during the fostering phase and when the child becomes subject to adoption regulations, early permanence is more widely used. A more detailed consideration is made later in this book, in Chapter 6.

To support the understanding of early permanence as a concept and how FfA fits within this, more joint training would be helpful for all professionals in the child care arena. Where agencies have been proactive in developing multi-disciplinary training materials and offering briefing sessions, there appears to be more willingness to be innovative about early permanence, such as by involving birth parents in the planning process.

THE ROLE AND INFLUENCE OF THE COURTS

It was acknowledged by the National Adoption Leadership Board in 2014 that, as a consequence of the *Re B* and *Re BS* rulings, there has been a decrease in the number of placement and adoption orders being made.* Some local authorities have also reported that their local courts have been more reluctant to accept the local authority's care plan for adoption or to make placement orders till they are satisfied that all other options have been fully explored. At the same time, there has been an increase in the number of special guardianship orders being made.

One of the identified barriers to FfA has been that some courts do not support early permanence placements on the basis that FfA is seen to disadvantage the birth parents.

It is well established in law that the courts do not have the power to direct a local authority to make a particular placement, so they may not direct that a child be found an FfA placement, or that a child be placed in a traditional foster placement when the local authority care plan proposes otherwise. The court can, however, ask (not order) the local authority to reconsider their care plan or can make an order for residential assessment of the child. We were advised that in some cases, courts were more inclined to direct that children be placed in parent and child assessment placements, rather than considering FfA. In contrast, we were also advised that in areas where early permanence had been discussed as part of Family Justice Board training and development, there was greater agreement about making FfA placements. In our contact with agencies, Gloucestershire County Council informed us that they had provided information sessions for their local CAFCASS and judiciary, and that this had had a beneficial effect in early permanence placements. These views were replicated across our focus group discussions.

* For more information on the rulings, visit www.bailii.org/uk/cases/UKSC/2013/33.html and www.familylawweek.co.uk/site.aspx?i=ed117048.

Where the judiciary is not apparently supportive of adoption in general and early permanence through FfA or concurrent planning in particular, it is important that the local authority provides clear evidence of the long-lasting impact that neglect and trauma can have on the child and how early permanence can mitigate against this. It is therefore essential that pre-birth assessments are robust enough to provide the evidence to convince a court that FfA is the most suitable plan for the child.

The following example outlines where things did not go according to the original plan due to lack of evidence:

> *The way the actual timings happened was that after two weeks, there was a hearing at which the birth mother took back her original consent to the placement with foster carers, and requested a residential assessment. Due to a lack of pre-birth planning... there was not enough information available for the judge to deny this request. I can't remember precisely, but effectively from then on they were looking for a suitable placement for the birth mother to go into, first to work with the assessment team whilst having contact at that unit with R, and then if all was going well (i.e. if the unit felt that it was viable to assess and no immediate safety issues), a hearing would then confirm the move of R into the unit for assessment. All in all, there were about six weeks when we knew he was likely to go but not definite.* (FfA4)

An example of evidence is set out in the report, *Improving the Life Chances of Children: A model for intervention-led pre-birth assessments* (Greenwood and McGregor, 2011), which explores a project targeted at families within Durham where a previous child was permanently removed from their care and either placed for adoption or with other family members. Early identification of families was key and action then involved a "team around the child". The authors concluded:

> *Children's life chances are greatly enhanced the earlier they are placed in families who can fully meet their needs. The longer children are exposed to the damaging effects of emotional abuse and neglect, the more difficult it becomes for the children to respond positively, as permanent changes in the brain fundamentally affect the child's ability to form secure attachments.*

Social workers are made aware of this report in the Early Permanence Resource Pack (Leeds City Council).

We would suggest that to support the ongoing development of early permanence practice, providing feedback to the Family Justice Boards of successful placements would be helpful. At the Inaugural Bridget Lindley Memorial lecture in March 2017, Lord Justice McFarlane commented on the lack of feedback offered to the judiciary following the making of adoption orders.

> *Magistrates and judges up and down the country on every day of the week are making these highly intrusive draconian orders removing children permanently from their natural families on the basis that to do so is better for the child and that "nothing else will do". But, I ask rhetorically: 'How do we know this is so?'*

He further commented that, 'Family judges receive almost no feedback on the outcome of the decisions that they make' (and therefore about placement success), and he wanted to see the research evidence showing that 'the stability and security provided by adoption is said to provide a quality of care which far outstrips any other model that might be available'.*

ROUTES TO PLACEMENT

As explored in Chapter 3, there are several ways of achieving early permanence. When social workers are considering FfA, they will need to be aware of the different possible routes to achieve this.

- In some agencies, it is generally expected that an FfA carer is already an approved adopter who has then received temporary approval from the local authority Nominated Officer for a named child (DfE, 2015, 25A). We look in more detail at the recruitment, preparation and assessment of FfA carers in the next chapter.
- In some agencies, prospective adopters are dually approved either by a permanence panel as foster carers and adopters, or through presentation first at an adoption panel and then a fostering panel.
- In some agencies, dually approved carers most often have children placed with them as concurrent planning placements, but in others they are taking FfA placements. As more local authorities develop their use of dual approval, this practice may increase.
- Some of the respondents to our questionnaire achieved early permanence with their children via concurrency, and their responses reflect the slightly different approach that their placements took.

> *As concurrent carers, we understood we were working with the local authority to achieve best outcomes for our daughter and that this may have included her returning to her birth family. Having researched childhood attachment, we firmly believed that the FfA option gives children the best chance of secure attachment outcomes.* (CP1)

* The typesecript of the lecture is available at: www.judiciary.gov.uk/wp-content/uploads/2017/03/transcript-the-inaugural-bridget-lindley-annual-memorial-lecture-march2017.pdf.

- Other respondents had taken the FfA route and were involved at the early stage of implementation of this new route to early permanence:

  > *Our social worker mentioned that they were interested in doing FfA and explained they may possibly have an unborn baby in mind to trial it with us as a first case. She mentioned it on a number of occasions and we liked the idea of it... FfA was right for us because we really wanted to put the child first and FfA did that. FfA meant that [our child] didn't have multiple moves and multiple people learning how to care for his needs after a difficult start to life.* (FfA8)

- In our focus groups, it became clear that some agencies are using Reg. 24 (2010) where a sibling or half-sibling of a previously adopted child comes into care. This was discussed in a previous chapter and should only be used where a child has been born and there has been insufficient time to complete an adoption assessment of the receiving family.

  It was recognised that this scenario can place adoptive families under significant pressure. It may not have been the family's plan to be re-approved at this stage and they may feel under duress to agree to take a sibling. It is vital that a full discussion is had prior to any placement being progressed to understand how the first child has settled, what routines he or she is in and how things may be disrupted by the arrival of a new baby. This is considered in more detail in Chapter 6.

  Given the inherent uncertainties of FfA placements, thought needs to be given as to how the adults and any other child in placement might manage the loss and change if a return to the birth family was to result. In some cases, agencies clearly feel that this is too risky an option and would therefore suggest that the new baby be placed with temporary foster carers until the family has had a chance to prepare the existing child. Some adopters have also taken this decision themselves and have asked for the new child to have a few weeks in foster care so that they can make the adjustments necessary to increasing their family.

THE POSITION OF BIRTH PARENTS

In considering which children may be appropriately placed in early permanence, it is important to think about the birth parents.

> *Parents do not set out to be bad parents and should be provided with an intensive planned intervention, assessment and support to help them.*
>
> (Summary of a model for intervention-led pre-birth assessments, Greenwood and McGregor, 2011)

Relinquishing a child

The term "relinquished baby" is used to describe a child under the age of six weeks whose birth parents are making the choice of adoption for the child. Statutory adoption guidance sets out the process to be followed in the case of relinquished babies under the age of six weeks, explored further in CAFCASS guidance (2013).

The process of relinquishment is based on the supposition that the agency or another professional is approached at an early stage by an expectant mother with the intention to relinquish her child and that this decision does not waver. However, experience has shown that the reality does not always match the expectation. Pregnancies are often concealed, birth mothers do not approach agencies at an early stage and will then frequently change their minds about relinquishing.

The balance between the right of the birth mother to request adoption and the right of the child to be brought up within his or her birth family is often challenging for social workers. Nevertheless, it is clear that the local authority is under a duty to do whatever it can to ensure that children are brought up within their birth family if at all possible, and that the child's welfare must be paramount in all its considerations.

The focus of local authorities' work with relinquishing birth mothers is based on the principle that adoption is a service for children and not for adults. Whilst the circumstances of mothers who have expressed a wish for their baby to be adopted must be carefully and sensitively considered, every effort will be made to explore the possibility of a parent caring for their child, or of the child being cared for within the extended family.

In our focus groups, there were several examples given where relinquished children had been placed with identified FfA carers and there had been complications during placement. Examples included birth mothers changing their minds about adoption or disengaging with the process prior to formal consent being given, leading to the need to apply for a court order; or not disclosing information about birth fathers, which led to the need to consult legal services, and in some cases, in which courts had become involved in ruling on whether fathers or family members should be contacted and their views sought, matters became protracted causing distress to the FfA carers and delay in achieving an adoption placement/order.

In cases of relinquishment, the social worker needs to spend significant time and effort with the birth parents, counselling them about the process ahead. The social worker and health professionals should give clear information and be able to answer the birth parents' questions about what will happen during the birth, after the child is delivered and over the next six weeks before a final decision is made with a CAFCASS officer. Where there is doubt that the birth parent understands the process, then efforts should be made to seek appropriate help, for example, interpreters, specialist legal advice, etc.

It is worth noting that having early pre-birth planning meetings with potential relinquishing birth parents is key in trying to ensure that birth parents fully understand their own position and the actions being planned by the local authority, and may help to iron out some of the potential post-placement difficulties. Comprehensive guidance is offered by CAFCASS (2013) in working with birth parents who have difficulties understanding the process:

> *3.20 If the AA [adoption agency] is aware at an early stage that issues of competency may require further considerations, they should not request a CAFCASS officer to witness consent until full enquiries have been completed. The AA must be sure that the parent or guardian is competent to give consent.*

In care proceedings

Where an FfA placement is being considered and may be viable, it is crucial that birth parents are consulted about their understanding of the situation and their views. This is enshrined in the Care Planning, Placement and Case Review Guidance 2015, that states that the responsible authority should:

> *As far as reasonably practicable ascertain the wishes and feelings of the child, his parent, any person who is not a parent of his but had parental responsibility for him and any other person whose wishes and feelings the authority considers to be relevant. (para 2.31)*

Where the local authority has identified that the likelihood of the child returning to their birth parents is very small and placement with FfA carers is in the child's best interests, the birth parents must be advised that the local authority cannot pre-judge the outcome of care proceedings, and only the court can authorise placement for adoption if they do not give consent to their child being placed for adoption. They should understand that they do not have a veto on this.

Statutory Guidance (DfE, 2015) notes that the care plan is critical and influential in the court's decision making:

> *While there is no requirement for a formal agreement by the parent to the court care plan, the responsible authority will be aware of the principles underpinning Article 8 of the European Convention on Human Rights (ECHR) concerning the "right to respect for family life" and should ensure that parents are appropriately consulted and that the reasons why their views have or have not been acted upon are recorded. (para 2.39)*

It is vital that social workers make robust efforts to ensure that during pre-proceedings, birth parents are given the opportunity to put forward any other relatives or connected persons who may be able to care for the child. These parties should then be fully assessed and either ruled in or out. A Family Group Conference at a very early stage is recommended and is mentioned in some of the policies and procedures we had access to during our discussions with agencies and in focus groups.

> *Social services did not contact all connected people at the outset and a few months into FfA, the court advised the social worker that these people should be contacted. These people wanted to be put forward to care for our child which caused us a huge amount of distress and upset. The birth father also came forward to care for our child after many months in placement.* (FfA6)

It is acknowledged that this process can be extremely challenging for birth parents, some of whom cannot understand the legal discussions that are held with them and about them. In circumstances where birth parents' comprehension is compromised or where English may not be their first language, they should have access to expert guidance to ensure that they understand that legal planning is on the side of their child. Where the court considers that the care plan for adoption and application for a placement order is an interference in the parent's rights under Article 6 or 8 of the European Convention on Human Rights, an alternative plan will be necessary.

In some of the questionnaire feedback, respondents reported various reactions from the birth parents of the children in question.

> *We had regular contact with the birth family which is a real positive of the adoption. In the end, it was a comfort to our daughter's birth mother to know the family she was adopted by. And we are able to talk to our daughter fully and freely about her birth family.* (CP1)

> *Initially they were very pleased that the baby was going to be placed with her siblings. And they thought of us as "friends" (their words). Once solicitors were involved that changed and they tried to make us out to be bad parents (hence the allegation). Once they had been assessed further and deemed to be unable to parent the baby adequately, they switched back to being happy that she was going to be placed with us for adoption.* (FfA1)

> *Initially the birth mother did not to meet us, as she was contesting the interim care order and then the placement order. That said, she was more content in the knowledge that our son would stay with us if it were to convert into an adoption. The birth father was not in the picture... We met the birth mother soon after the placement order was granted. It was a massively positive experience for everyone involved.* (FfA3)

From feedback, it is clear that although early permanence is an excellent option for the child, it can be challenging and upsetting for birth parents and at times for adopters, and that these placements require the services of confident and experienced workers to establish co-operative working relationships.

Guidance for birth parents has been designed by a number of agencies and Essex County Council has shared their leaflet with us (see Appendix 7). There is also a useful Family Rights Group Advice Sheet for birth parents involved in care proceedings where adoption is likely to be the plan (Family Rights Group, 2014b).

Where information has been shared in an open and transparent way, some birth parents have been more able to accept early permanence:

> *I liked the carers when I first met them... They kept a diary for me of the baby's sleeping and feeding. They showed me the diary whenever we had contact. Later I wrote to the judge saying that the baby could be adopted only if he could go to the carers, as I know they will love him.*
>
> (Leeds City Council, 2015)

As part of our discussions with agencies, we have been keen to establish in what other ways birth parents can be encouraged to participate fully in the plans for their children. This is explored fully earlier in this chapter. However, it is worth noting that some agencies are developing a proactive approach to involving birth parents at an early stage. CCS Adoption has funding to:

> *...pilot a mediation service for birth parents and early permanence carers called Sharing Stories to assist communication throughout the period when contact is taking place. It is envisaged that enhanced communication will help all parties in the process and greatly benefit the child by improving information sharing, which will lay the foundations for enhanced life story work. The potential value of involving birth parents in early life story work cannot be underestimated as robust life story work/information underpins the stability of permanence placements for children. The project will offer a service across the Adoption West Regional Adoption Agency area.*
>
> (*Early Permanence News*, February 2017, www.adoptionconcurrency.org)

PRE-PLACEMENT MATCHING CONSIDERATIONS

The matching panel and post-placement considerations are covered more fully later in this book, but it is important to consider how agencies are "matching" children to FfA carers prior to making the placement. We have been provided with a number of tools that different agencies are using to support making the link between an approved adopter/FfA carer and their family and a child. Where a family is dually approved, it remains important to consider the specific skills and qualities they have that mean this could be a positive link. There are various proformas that have been developed with similar aims and that focus on the known and predicted needs of the child and the skills and potential capacities of the adopters to meet these. Issues such as health (of both parties), location, background factors (again, of both parties), flexibility to take the child at short notice with an understanding of the expectations of being a foster carer, are all considered at this point. The availability of these FfA carers to meet the contact needs of the child must also form part of this process. Other issues will include any relating to the support networks of the prospective carers and their commitments to other children. If the agency decision-maker or Nominated Officer feels that there is enough evidence to recommend temporary approval as foster carers for this specific child, then the placement will be made.

CHECKLIST FOR PRACTITIONERS

- Ensure that legal protocols are followed in all cases.
- Be clear that birth parents are involved and consulted.
- Ensure that FfA carers are fully briefed about the circumstances of the case.
- Give appropriate paperwork to the FfA carers.
- Ensure that all professionals involved in the case are clear about confidentiality, roles and responsibilities.

Chapter 6

Recruitment, preparation, assessment and approval of Fostering for Adoption carers

Since the Government amended the Care Planning, Placement and Case Review Regulations to include FfA (Reg. 25a) in 2013, it is expected that local authorities and VAAs will ensure that FfA is a consideration for all children with a care plan for adoption and for all prospective adopters. This chapter focuses on the processes involving prospective adopters.

It became clear from our discussions with agencies and from information we received via our questionnaire that practice in the recruitment, preparation and assessment of FfA carers across the country is variable and in differing stages of development. The following quotes demonstrate some of the views of our contributors.

> *I think a training day we attended was a little bit helpful (although retrospectively not entirely!). We had read things from [our agency] and heard about FfA in the news. I think figuring out what that would mean for us we mostly did ourselves, but we were also asked about it during our assessment process to an extent.* (FfA4)

> *We had been introduced to someone who had already been through the concurrent caring process and had very open and honest discussions with them before attending open evenings and further discussions.* (FfA5)

RECRUITMENT OF FfA CARERS

Recruitment of adopters has traditionally varied geographically depending on the needs identified in the location. For sibling groups needing adoption, agencies often devised specific recruitment campaigns reflecting the needs of children waiting. Similar campaigns have been launched to encourage applications from people interested in parenting children with complex physical or medical needs, children from a BME or dual heritage background, or older children who have traditionally been seen as "hard to place". Since the Adoption and

Children Act 2002 amendments, recruitment activity has often been shared across adoption consortia to try and maximise enquiries. There was a significant increase in the number of prospective adopters between 2010 and 2014 that led to many people waiting for the child whom they felt they could parent. In response, some agencies have felt cautious about recruiting more prospective adopters for what was seen as a diminishing number of children with a care plan for adoption. In 2017, adoption agencies in England are facing new challenges as RAAs are developing and it is clear from our focus groups that adopter recruitment is high on the agenda of these new organisations, and that targeted recruitment is planned, including specific campaigns for the above groups and FfA carers.

It is essential that other parts of children's services are familiar with the concept of early permanence in order to support these placements effectively. As well as preparing prospective adopters, we learned that some agencies have been extremely proactive in providing training and guidance for their child care and fostering colleagues, IROs and CAFCASS workers.

As RAAs become operational, it will be crucial that, in order to facilitate successful FfA placements, the systems established enable collaborative work to continue between those holding adoption knowledge in the RAA and the child care practitioners and legal services in the local authority.

Agencies have shared some of the materials they use to promote FfA with their prospective adopters and it is clear that FfA is being featured in their publicity materials and discussed from the time of the initial enquiry. Derbyshire County Council, for example, offers all prospective adopters a range of materials including a brochure dedicated to early permanence via FfA (2016). The quotes below are taken from this:

> ***Why Fostering for Adoption?***
>
> *FfA protects children from experiencing numerous moves within the care system. It provides children with good quality uninterrupted care while assessments of their birth family are completed and the court decides on the best plan for the child. Consistent care reduces possible future harm and helps the child develop healthy attachments.*
>
> ***What are the benefits for the carer?***
>
> *FfA carers have the immense satisfaction of providing stability and security for the child at an early stage, with the possibility that he or she may become their legally adopted child if agreed by the court. FfA carers receive thorough preparation and training during assessment and post-approval.*

Northamptonshire County Council provides information on their adoption website and makes it clear that:

> *An FfA placement will only be made where there is clear evidence to the local authority that there is very little likelihood that the birth parents can resolve their problems or that other family members can take care of the child. The evidence will need to be substantial and this usually means that the parents have had other children placed for adoption and their circumstances have not changed for the birth of their new child. There may be other circumstances where FfA might apply but the evidence will still need to be substantial.*
>
> (Northamptonshire County Council, 2016)

It is expected that all adoption agencies will provide information to all prospective adopters about early permanence, identifying the benefits to children and adoptive families as well as some of the potential risks involved. It is good practice to ensure that prospective adopters have a range of options to consider at an early stage so that they can be encouraged to do their own research during Stage One of the assessment process. Agency websites should provide accurate legal information, some case examples (including film footage, where possible), comments from experienced FfA adopters, birth parents and other professionals who have had involvement in these cases. Southampton City Council, for example, has a clip on YouTube that explores the concept of early permanence: www.youtube.com/watch?v=cAZWECi2wPQ.

In addition, directing prospective adopters to First4Adoption and DirectGov websites is helpful, as both sites offer practical information about the realities of taking a child in this way, including adoption pay and leave arrangements. Ideally, recruitment materials should give legal information in a clear and focused manner and reflect the circumstances in which early permanence placements are most successful for all parties. As part of the recruitment process, it is envisaged that adoption teams will work collaboratively with colleagues in the fostering service to involve them in supporting the adoption team to ensure that prospective adopters are given clear guidance on the expectations of them as foster carers.

Some agencies already have a fostering manager or practitioner attend their information events to discuss the realities of roles and responsibilities, daily logs and contact issues, and other issues that may impact on the FfA placement. This seems to be an excellent way of working alongside colleagues and ensuring that there is consistency of practice.

This is then followed by the provision of mentors during Stage One, when applicants can access an experienced FfA carer to explore issues in more detail.

We would suggest that a basic leaflet outlining some of the main expectations of FfA carers whilst fostering should be included in the recruitment pack.

Best practice in the recruitment of FfA carers would include:

- robust publicity materials, both online and in hard copy, and appropriately targeted at local communities;
- clear and confident presentations by knowledgeable workers at information events (preferably including fostering colleagues);
- reference to case examples throughout the preparation training, with access to adopters who have been through the process (either successfully achieving adoption, or where complications had arisen); and
- information on statutory adoption pay and leave arrangements, fostering allowances, early support and post-placement support.

> *To us, it was not the only route we had considered to building a family. However, we did see it as a high risk–reward option. We knew about the challenges involved, but we felt it would be an amazing start to our family if we were involved in our child's life from such an early point.* (FfA3)

> *The social worker provided information regarding adoption pay/leave and the fostering manager regarding the fostering allowance... We were provided with full details of responsibilities, including recording information, mandatory training courses, etc, by the fostering manager.* (FfA6)

CHECKLIST FOR PRACTITIONERS

- Include a specific focus on early permanence within the adoption recruitment strategy.
- Ensure that all staff responsible for recruitment are fully conversant with FfA as a potential route to adoption.
- Provide specific information on the agency website about early permanence (FfA in particular), including positive statements about the wide profile of such prospective adopters.
- Provide downloadable materials and information sheets for prospective carers and their relatives outlining the benefits of early permanence.
- Ensure that FfA is profiled at all information and recruitment events.
- Utilise experienced FfA adopters at these events.

PREPARATION OF FfA CARERS

It is evident that agencies already have different ways of preparing prospective adopters for FfA placements, and that as RAAs are developing, these will be adapted further. In our focus groups and discussions with adoption agencies, we have seen evidence of a range of excellent tools used in the early Stage One preparation courses that emphasise the benefits of FfA for children and highlight some of the potential risks for adopters.

Essex County Council uses a PowerPoint presentation (2016) in their preparation for early permanence, one slide of which lays out the challenges for prospective adopters very clearly:

- *The final outcome may not be adoption.*
- *Uncertainty about health and development.*
- *Likely to be at short notice with less opportunity for proper introductions or preparation.*
- *Additional expectations on carers during fostering stage.*
- *No matching decision until placement order is made.*
- *No shared parental responsibility until placement order is made.*
- *Early permanence might feel risky especially if you have already experienced many losses.*

Some agencies have adapted existing training materials to incorporate the historical and legislative background of early permanence, with a focus on either concurrency or FfA. Others have decided to provide additional training days after the basic preparation courses to focus specifically on early permanence, often using experienced FfA adopters to provide examples and experiences. Case studies are used effectively to highlight different aspects of the task and prospective adopters are asked to explore what they might do or how they might react in different situations.

Families for Children (South West) uses an additional workbook that is given to prospective adopters during their preparation (see Appendix 8). The strength of this workbook is that it asks the prospective adopters at an early stage to explore their motivation for considering FfA, and to focus on the skills and attributes they might bring to caring for a child in these circumstances. It also asks applicants to think about the stresses of managing uncertainty and potential loss. It makes sense to allow prospective adopters time and space at an early stage to consider the potential impact of early permanence on themselves, any other children in the family and their extended networks before expecting them to make a definite decision about whether or not to pursue FfA.

The preparation of potential FfA adopters would include all the general topics associated with adoption training. Courses will incorporate sessions on the legislative framework surrounding looked after children and adoption, the type of children who require substitute families and may have a care plan for adoption, and the family background issues that lead to these conclusions. To ensure that FfA features in these sessions, it is recommended that training materials are fully updated to include examples of children placed under dual approval or Reg. 25a, with clear guidance on how these placements are set up and what the role and responsibility of the FfA carer will be.

A glossary of terms that includes some of the legal terminology used in care proceedings should be part of a preparation pack.

Health and developmental issues

Preparation of adopters focuses very much on the potential needs of children placed away from their birth families, including the impact of early trauma and how this may affect the children throughout their lives. Given that many of the FfA placements involve very young babies and toddlers where substance misuse, domestic violence and neglect may have been features of their early days (including in utero), training for FfA carers should include the possibility of parenting children where very little is known about the birth family and where developmental uncertainty is a likelihood. Training should also encourage them to consider what strengths and resilience they may have to manage this level of uncertainty.

The realities of caring for very young babies who have been born with neonatal abstinence syndrome should be covered in all training for adopters, as should other elements of child development and child health, but with FfA carers this is essential. It is likely that families who put themselves forward for early permanence placements will be called on at fairly short notice to consider potential placements and there may be scant information available. Good practice therefore is to offer these aspects of training prior to the arrival of a child. We are aware of several agencies that have some mandatory post-approval courses that include paediatric first aid, caring for children with complex health needs and the potential impact of foetal alcohol spectrum disorders.

Qualities of prospective FfA carers

Agencies should be looking for qualities such as: emotional warmth; stability and security; physical and emotional availability; inclusivity; flexibility and adaptability in all adopters, but for FfA carers it is most important that the adults can demonstrate the capacity to put the child first at all times. They will need to have capacity to manage risk, deal with issues of loss, and accept that they will be in situations where they are not in control of the outcome.

The Secure Base Model, devised by Beek and Schofield (2004; see also Schofield and Beek, 2014a, 2014b), is an excellent tool that is often used in the training of foster carers and could also be used during adopter preparation to encourage applicants to think about the skills and attributes that are likely to enhance their parenting. This model can be particularly useful in helping FfA carers to consider how they manage the potential difficulties of "sharing" the child with the birth parent during the fostering phase:

- *Providing availability: the carer's ability to convey a strong sense of availability to meet the child's needs, even when they are apart from the child.*
- *Promoting reflective capacity: the carer's capacity to think sensitively about what is happening in the mind of the child and to reflect this back to the child.*

(Beek and Schofield, 2004, p 135)

FfA carers must be able to recognise that at the point of placement they are foster carers, not adopters, and that "sharing" the child is inevitable unless that child is relinquished and their parent/s have withdrawn.

Preparation of adopters will also include sessions on child development and the promotion of attachment behaviours. For FfA carers, it is essential that they are given the opportunity to consider how they may have to manage a child exposed to differing parenting styles and strategies during the fostering phase and what impact this may have on the child. Several practitioners we heard from commented on the difficulties experienced by FfA and concurrent carers of having to manage children returning from contact sessions where birth parents had handled the child in a different way to how they would have done, had fed the child foods that they wouldn't have given them and had generally provided a variable standard of care.

It is accepted that preparing people for these tasks can feel hypothetical and that the reality is very different. However, preparation courses must incorporate these issues. This is an area where the inclusion of experienced FfA adopters in the training sessions is invaluable.

> *Once she was born, we waited two days whilst the placement was confirmed before picking her up from hospital. It's certainly true to say that however well prepared we were intellectually, nothing had prepared us for the emotional impact of caring for a vulnerable newborn just separated from her birth mother – and the emotional strain of the possibility of her returning to a potentially dangerous situation.* (CP1)

Once he was with us, it all felt very different and I don't think you can stress this difference enough to parents considering this route. (FfA3)

PREPARATION FOR THE FOSTERING ROLE

Additional topics that must be covered during FfA preparation include significant information about the fostering role and the expectations that the agency will have. Issues such as how delegated authority is managed are important as, during the fostering phase, the FfA carers will not share parental responsibility with the local authority.

Clarity about what FfA carers can and cannot do must be laid out as part of their initial preparation. We heard from workers that this was an area that could cause some confusion, such as in relation to the names used by FfA carers who were not clear what they should call themselves to the child. Using "Mum" and "Dad" was evidently problematic whilst the child was still having contact with birth parents but would also be pre-empting the outcome of the court.

We also heard that it was hard for FfA carers to manage the knowledge that the child could return home and to think about how they should deal with this, particularly with their own relatives and other children in the home. This is where involving existing foster carers and experienced FfA carers in preparation can be of real benefit. CSS Adoption has provided us with a useful leaflet that they give to relatives of FfA carers, and has been included in this guide as Appendix 9.

Support for FfA carers during fostering

The provision of placement support is covered more fully in the next chapter, but takes on specific significance for FfA carers. As prospective foster carers, all FfA carers need to be made aware of the agency's policies and that they will be entitled to a fostering allowance throughout the fostering phase.

This provision of fostering payments is another area that, in the development of an RAA, will need to be thought through so that there is consistency across all their member agencies.

During Stage One of the adopter assessment and as part of their preparation, we would suggest that the adoption agency advises prospective adopters that they involve their employers in early discussions about how they might be supported, including through statutory adoption pay and leave, if they take an early permanence placement. Those interested in pursuing early permanence must have clear information on who will support them and how, and what implications there may be if they choose not to take s.22C adoption leave when the child is placed as an FfA placement.

If the agency is solely registered as a VAA, there may be no access to fostering workers, so how will this support be managed and by whom? If they are to be supported by their assessing social worker, what input will there be from the local authority fostering service? Prospective adopters must have clarity about who will provide the supervision and support during the fostering phase, what will be required of them in terms of written records, safer caring, etc, and how they can access guidance and advice. This is an area that requires careful planning and collaboration on the part of adoption agencies where interagency placements are being made. It will also be a topic for discussion as RAA practice is being developed.

Other household members

Guidance and advice about how to involve other household members (birth children and other adopted children in particular) and extended family form part of all adopter preparation and it is good practice to offer training either as part of the initial preparation course or as an add-on post-approval. Some agencies have devised specific "related by adoption" sessions that are designed to give grandparents and other close relatives an opportunity to consider the differences between birth parenting and parenting via adoption. The book *Related by Adoption* (Argent, 2014) contains useful advice. CCS Adoption has prepared some written guidance, included in this guide as Appendix 9. These opportunities will be highly significant in the preparation of FfA carers and we would suggest that all relatives should have the opportunity to understand more about FfA and the fostering task that the carers will be managing and how this varies from a traditional adoption placement. This might be an area in which RAAs can come together to have joint regional training sessions for family members and relatives.

Adopters all need a robust support network, but the additional emotional uncertainty of FfA placements means that their close friends and family need to be able to provide the right type of advice and support.

> *Trying to keep the wider family at bay and not get too attached to our son was also a challenge as they were genuinely delighted we had a child at last and were so excited about having a baby in the family. We tried to remind people often of the risks associated with the placement and that permanence was not guaranteed.* (FfA3)

Children in the family will require specific preparation, and for some of our contributors this evidently presented some challenges.

> *In retrospect, I think we totally failed our [existing] daughter about trying to prepare her for concurrent planning and how it might be once a foster*

> *sibling arrived. I think we were too hung up on the detail of concurrent planning to understand that for a four-year-old, the arrival of another child is about the shift out of the limelight for them – which all first borns experience.* (CP4)

> *Our existing children were not provided with the full story – we couldn't allow there to be any doubt that the baby would be staying, as they wouldn't be able to deal with the uncertainty very well. We therefore let them know their birth parents were having another baby and that we had the option of her joining our family. For the children, it therefore felt like a family decision which they were involved in.* (FfA1)

> *We told our youngest child that we were going to look after a baby whilst the social worker found a new mummy and daddy for him. We did this to protect her in case the situation arose that a care order/plan for adoption would not be the decision that was made. We told our older daughter everything as she was an older teen at the time and had a greater level of understanding.* (FfA2)

Coram and BAAF (2013) recognised that the age and understanding of other children in the family will be very important in determining what they will be told of the planned placement. Children already in the family should be included in discussion and planning, consistent with their age and understanding, with the outcome and issues from this work identified in the relevant reports to the panel or agency decision-maker.

Workers need to have these discussions with adopters considering offering an FfA placement who have birth children or have previously adopted siblings of the child, and explore their views on what their children will be able to understand or cope with. Where the parents do not feel able to be open with their child/ren about the full circumstances of the situation, they should be encouraged to think through all the possible outcomes of the placement and how subsequently these would be explained to their children if, for example, the child then remains and is revealed as their sibling or returns to a birth family carer.

CHECKLIST FOR PRACTITIONERS

- Involve adopters who have offered FfA placements and foster carers on training courses.
- Use varied and relevant case scenarios that explore all aspects of FfA placements – the successes and those that do not proceed to adoption.
- Ensure that all trainers are fully conversant with the legislation surrounding early permanence and that they give a balanced view of the process.

- Training materials should include a glossary of terms to make sense of the legal process.
- Include information about statutory adoption pay and leave.
- Provide clear guidance about roles and responsibilities of foster carers, training, allowances and support, and what will happen if a child is returned to the care of their birth family.
- Provide access to buddies or mentors.
- Ensure that relatives of the FfA carers have access to training and information.
- Give specific thought and planning as to how existing children of the FfA carers will be helped to understand the nature of the placement.

ASSESSMENT OF FfA CARERS

Most adoption agencies use the CoramBAAF Prospective Adopter's Report (PAR) when assessing adopters, and the 2016 version now incorporates sections that relate specifically to early permanence. The guidance notes attached to the PAR 2016 are extremely thorough and offer suggestions as to how the additional requirements of FfA can be included in the report. *Undertaking an Adoption Assessment in England* (Dibben, 3rd edn, 2017), is a comprehensive general guide to completing the PAR and assists the assessor in taking a methodical approach to the process.

Stage Two of the adoption assessment is very much led by the adoption worker, with an expectation that the training, reading and research undertaken by adopters in Stage One will enhance the process. If FfA has been thoroughly incorporated into the recruitment and preparation process, the prospective adopters should already have some idea of what they might be offering and how this will need to be explored during the assessment and evidenced in the report. Below, we look at some specific issues particular to the assessment of FfA carers.

Individual profile and family and environmental factors

Adoption assessments require a comprehensive exploration of each applicant, looking at family background, health and education as well as previous relationships and employment. From these discussions, evidence from referees and from social work observations, it is anticipated that the assessor can comment on aspects of resilience and the prospective adopter's capacity to recognise, understand and manage stress. This has particular resonance when considering the skills and capacities needed in early permanence placements.

As we have seen from some of our FfA carers' comments, FfA placements can be immensely stressful and the adoption agency must be confident that the prospective adopters are robust and insightful enough for the challenges ahead and that they have a strong and practical support network to lean on at difficult moments.

They were very supportive. They all understood what was at stake, and were very concerned for us throughout the whole process. They were great at reminding us that it was not all doom and gloom, despite it all being so uncertain. They played an important role for us, we think. (FfA3)

I think after [our first child] went back it was hard at times for people to know what to say as it was very sad for us... That also meant that I think people felt with [our second child] they needed to be cautious and didn't quite know when to be happy about it. (FfA4)

Assessments should include short examples of how the prospective adopters have managed difficulties in their lives, how they cope with unplanned changes and how they have been able to negotiate times when they have felt powerless or out of control. These examples have a particular poignancy for FfA where the final decisions lie with the court and may prove emotionally challenging for the FfA carer. It would be helpful for the assessing worker to have access to examples of FfA placements that have gone according to the care plan and some that have not, so that more realistic and in-depth discussions can take place.

Having gathered factual information, verification and observations, the assessor must then make sense of this and analyse how the prospective adopter is likely to cope under pressure, how flexible and adaptable they are, and what skills they may bring to the fostering as well as the parenting task.

Where there are existing birth children, step-children or other adopted children living within the FfA home, the assessor will need to consider references from schools, health professionals, etc. These external views may give insight into how emotionally robust the child or children are and on what developmental level they are functioning. As has already been suggested, the arrival of a younger child in the family can have quite an impact, particularly where there is the uncertainty of whether they will remain in the longer term, and the assessor needs to have a broader understanding of this so that they can work with the FfA adopters to undertake appropriate work with the child in question. There must also be clarity about what child care arrangements for existing children may be needed to facilitate the additional demands of an FfA placement, especially contact.

Foster families with birth children can offer good advice on how they have approached the "uncertainty" issue, and we would suggest that during the assessment there is a time when prospective adopters considering FfA can talk through with an experienced foster carer or

FfA carer some of the potential challenges they may face with their children if the FfA placement is problematic. A one-off training slot in the preparation group is unlikely to be sufficient; rather, an ongoing dialogue with a "buddy" or mentor is likely to make these sections of the assessment process more meaningful and will provide evidence for the final report.

Becoming adopters: the assessment of adoptive parenting

Understanding the motivation to adopt is crucial to the assessment process and prospective adopters need to be able to discuss their "journey" coherently and openly. Where infertility has been part of their motivation, it is essential when considering FfA that this is covered in significant detail during the assessment, and that the PAR captures how the applicants have managed this and any implications for them if they have to manage the uncertainties of FfA.

> *We'd always wanted to be parents but for some unknown reason I kept miscarrying. We were advised to try IVF, which we did three times and I had a miscarriage each time. So we decided to give ourselves some time to grieve. The more we talked about it, the more we realised we really did want to be parents. We'd talked about adoption early on in our marriage and decided it was something we'd like to do once we'd had our own children. But when we realised we'd probably never do that, we decided we wanted to go ahead and adopt.* (FfA8)

> *Many infertile couples emphasise how the stresses upon themselves and their partners have served to demonstrate the strength of their relationship, whilst many others say that theirs has deepened and matured in the face of adversity. A good partnership bolsters self-esteem, which in itself is an important aid to surviving difficult times.*
>
> (Millar and Paulson-Ellis, 2009, p 22)

Adoption has always been a "risky business" in the sense that matches can sometimes not work out, but more recently there has been a greater level of uncertainty with more birth parents appealing following the placement order being made and at the stage of the adoption order application. This can evidently create emotional turmoil for adopters and previous feelings of loss and grief associated with infertility may return. With FfA placements, the higher levels of risk may prove too traumatic for some prospective adopters and during the assessment it is crucial that these issues are discussed openly. The assessor has the responsibility to ensure that prospective adopters are given full information about the risks and benefits associated with early permanence, and to ensure that adopters can recognise how their infertility may potentially impact on them during FfA. Where the assessment is that the uncertainty may be too difficult for adopters, this should be made clear in the PAR and an explanation offered as to how this conclusion was reached. Should prospective adopters wish to challenge an agency view on their suitability to take an early permanence placement, they would need to offer more evidence of how some of the very real uncertainties might be managed.

Infertility is not the only motivating factor for adoption and we received contributions from families where their faith was a factor, where same-sex couples had actively chosen adoption as a way of building a family, and from single applicants who very much wanted to be parents but did not feel that medical intervention was the right approach for them. In all these situations, early permanence was an option discussed with them and formed part of the information provided in their PAR.

Within the PAR, there is always an exploration with prospective adopters about their expectations of the child whom they hope to adopt, their expectations and understanding of the role of adoptive parents, their understanding of the lifelong nature of adoption and how this may impact on the child's identity, and what they feel they have to offer as parents. In addition, the assessment of FfA carers demands that the assessor spends time considering the fostering task and how this might impact on family life. Assessors will often use a "day in the life" exercise or a "week in the life" with prospective adopters and this can be an extremely graphic way of enabling applicants to see what commitments they may have with an FfA placement. This includes contact appointments, health appointments, review meetings, daily logs, etc, alongside the already busy schedule of being a new parent who is getting to know the child, and can provide a reality check.

Do these prospective adopters have the time and emotional energy to give to the fostering task? If these exercises are completed early on in the assessment process, this then gives applicants and their extended families/support networks an opportunity to consider very carefully the realities of FfA and what additional support the applicants may require to sustain them. Again, this needs to be evidenced in the PAR and the strengths and vulnerabilities identified.

It is particularly important within the assessment process that the prospective adopters understand that early permanence placements not only come with risks around whether or not adoption will be the final plan, but that the child may not come with full background information, particularly where it is not known at this early stage. Assessors need to be reassured about the prospective adopters' understanding of the potential implications of genetic factors, of the impact on a child of being exposed to alcohol and drugs in utero and the many other issues that arise for looked after children.

What is the applicants' attitude towards health and potential disability? Have they any experience of learning disability or mental health conditions? These again are questions asked of all prospective adopters, but take on significance when early permanence is being considered.

Where the applicants identify that they feel they can consider a child from a different ethnic background from their own, this evidently needs considerable exploration in the PAR. Given that some FfA placements involve very young babies where there is perhaps little information on the heritage or nationality of the birth father, this is an issue that must be carefully considered with the prospective adopters. Dibben (2017, p 41) highlights the following information that needs to be explored:

- *Is there evidence that the applicant has non-discriminatory attitudes and values?*
- *Has the applicant had any personal experience that might help them care for a child from a different ethnicity or a disabled child?*
- *Are there people in their family and friends network who could help the applicant if they were adopting a child from a different cultural, ethnic or religious background?*
- *Were there family members with discriminatory attitudes? And if so, has the applicant given thought to how they would deal with this and is the assessor satisfied that this will not expose children to negative experiences?*
- *Does the assessor feel confident that this is a family that would challenge prejudice in an appropriate way if it arose?*

Fast-track assessments

Many FfA placements are made with families who already have one or more siblings (or half-siblings) of the child in question. It is very often the case that the adopters have obtained an adoption order for the children already in the family and therefore they are no longer "approved" adopters. Once the new child is discussed with them, it is anticipated that they would go through a "second-time adopter assessment" process. This would essentially involve updating the original PAR with more information, evidence and analysis of how they have adapted to being a family, what skills in child care they have developed, and what the needs of any children in the household may be. It is expected that fast-track assessments would take no more than four months.

However, as we have seen from some of our contributors, things can happen very quickly and rather than a child being placed in a mainstream foster placement whilst the adoption assessment is carried out, children have been placed under Reg. 24 Connected Person Regulations. This is not the recommended course of action, as previously discussed. We would strongly recommend that, where it is known that a birth family is expecting another child and that adoption is the likely care plan, a very early discussion is had with the adopters of the first child/ren so that an assessment can be started quickly, if that is what the prospective FfA family wants. They must be prepared that this will be a foster placement initially and that there is a high level of uncertainty attached. This is where networks between legal services, health professionals, child care teams and the adoption service need to be extremely robust.

In some situations, where adopters have one child in placement and a sibling arrives very quickly, it may not be appropriate to consider making an early permanence placement straight away. We are aware that some adopters have asked that the second child spends a short time in foster carer prior to coming to them so that they can prepare properly.

In one example, provided by Sheffield City Council, a couple had a young boy placed with them at 11 months, and his sister was born when he was just 14 months old. The family definitely wanted to take his sister, but instead of taking her as a "connected person", they asked if they could be re-assessed as adopters, in order to give their son a little more time to settle and bond with them. This was achieved and the sister was placed when she was aged two months and the brother was nearly 17 months. As a family, they felt much more prepared for this and felt that the young boy had coped well with the arrival of a sibling.

Practitioners must be aware of the pressure that some families might experience and realise that there needs to be flexibility in the process.

The role of the adoption panel when FfA is being considered

In all cases of PARs being presented to the adoption panel for a recommendation of being suitable to adopt, the worker should have presented information, evidence and analysis to support their recommendation. The adoption panel should be able to identify strengths and vulnerabilities in the applicants and be able to make a sensible and safe recommendation based on what is written. It is important to remind people that although applicants must be invited to attend the panel, they are not bound to appear. This therefore means that the PAR must be robust enough for the panel to feel confident in the knowledge, skills and attributes identified within the report and to make a recommendation. Indeed, even where applicants do attend, recommendation should be based on the paperwork and not their "performance".

Although the adoption panel remit is to consider the concept of "suitability" per se, where an assessor is additionally suggesting that the applicant has capacity to provide an FfA placement, a sibling placement or a transracial placement, the report must provide evidence of how the prospective adopters will manage the situation, both now and into the future. Where FfA is being considered, the relevant sections of the PAR should provide panel members with evidence and reassurance of how these issues have been addressed. We would suggest that in addition to training on FfA offered to other members of the child care profession, this should also be made available to adoption panel members, focusing very much on the fostering aspects of the task. It would seem logical to invite some fostering panel members or fostering social workers to attend this training in order that they can reflect on some of the evidence they look for in fostering assessments. Where the fostering panel is looking at fostering approval, those panel members will also need training on the role of FfA carers and expectations.

In the future, where adoption panels will be hosted by an RAA, they will need to consider carefully how to achieve consistency across all the participating agencies. It will also be an opportunity to share existing practice and learn from those agencies that are further forward in how they achieve early permanence. It is suggested that once RAAs are operational, a full training and development programme is offered, allowing all managers, workers and panels to become familiar with what will be the protocols of the RAA in relation to FfA and early permanence.

If the adoption panel has any concerns or there is confusion about why an applicant feels that they can offer an early permanence placement, these questions can be asked within the panel discussion and recorded within the minutes.

> *Each panel member should be asked whether he or she supports a proposed recommendation. Guidance 1.46 makes clear that: 'Where panel members have serious reservations, the panel Chair must ensure that these are recorded in the minutes and are attached to the panel's recommendations.'*
>
> (Lord and Cullen, 2016, p 15)

Lord and Cullen (2016, p 45) further note that:

> *Although there is no requirement for the panel to consider this information when recommending the suitability of the adopter for approval, the CoramBAAF PAR (2016) enables the assessing social worker to cover the information required for approval under Reg. 25a. As practice has developed in this area, panels have begun to address with applicants their understanding of and preparation for the role of an FfA carer and can then include advice about this to the agency decision-maker or Nominated Officer.*

The adoption panel can therefore include advice about suitability to offer an FfA placement alongside any advice about the age, number or sex of a child being placed.

It might be that a panel feels able to recommend that applicants are "suitable" to adopt, but finds that there is insufficient evidence about their suitability to offer an FfA placement. In these situations, the adoption panel may offer advice to the agency about providing further training or the services of a buddy or mentor prior to Reg. 25A approval being considered. To avoid such an outcome, it is important that, as part of the quality assurance process, the assessor and their manager ensure that the recommendation is supported by the information, evidence and analysis in the PAR.

The agency decision-maker will then receive the panel minutes and paperwork and will make their decision about suitability to adopt accordingly, and can also give advice about the applicants' ability to offer an FfA placement. In some agencies, the Nominated Officer who is asked to give the temporary fostering approval for an FfA placement will be the agency decision-maker; in others, it will be another senior manager. It is therefore vital that the evidence of strengths and capacities is readily available in the PAR and that the panel minutes and agency decision-maker reflect their views on this to assist the later decision-making process.

Permanence panels

To approve concurrent planning carers or FfA dually approved carers, agencies can use a permanency panel that is constituted to meet the requirements of both fostering and adoption regulations. In this way, the prospective adopter can be given dual approval by one panel. There are several different arrangements currently in the voluntary sector – some VAAs are also registered as a fostering service, e.g. Barnardos's, and can dual approve their carers for adoption *and* fostering. Some other VAAs have existing or proposed joint ventures so that the agency registered as a fostering service can provide the fostering approval, e.g. Caritas Care has a joint venture with Adoption Matters so that both agencies can approve their adopters, but Caritas Care makes the fostering approval. Also, Coram Cambridgeshire Adoption has specifically registered as a fostering service to provide concurrent fostering placements so that they can dual approve. This will be a consideration for RAAs as they look at how to establish their services.

Where dual approval is being sought, Lord and Cullen (2016, p 14) suggest that 'if an agency wishes to have some adopters also approved as foster carers... before a specific child has been identified for placement, an adoption and permanence panel able to consider both approvals would be likely to work best'.

Where a permanence panel is being used to dual approve applicants, it will be important that the minutes show that two separate recommendations have been made, as suitable to adopt and as suitable to foster, so that there is clarity about the legislation being used for each part of the recommendation. Some agencies would state the terms of the fostering recommendation, i.e. to offer concurrent or FfA placements only. If an age range is being proposed, it will be important to ensure that it covers any unforeseen delays in the process that may present after a child has been placed.

Where an FfA placement is to be considered with approved adopters from a VAA, the Nominated Officer in the placing local authority would then be responsible for agreeing their temporary fostering approval and they would become foster carers for that local authority.

Where an adoption and permanence panel is developed to consider dual approval, then it is essential that the Chair and central list panel members are fully briefed on the issues of early permanence generally and FfA in particular.

CHECKLIST FOR PRACTITIONERS

- Ensure that Stage One processes are robust and that they relate to Stage Two, i.e. references, information on other children, finances, etc.
- Revisit the guidance to the PAR (2016) whilst assessing adopters, focusing on how people have managed stress and uncertainty in their lives.
- Consider the use of the Secure Base Model to inform understanding of how available, inclusive and sensitive the applicants might be.
- Consider the range of uncertainties likely in early permanence so that applicants are clear about the potential risks.
- Use experienced FfA adopters as mentors during the assessment process.
- Ensure that adoption and/or permanence panels are fully briefed about the requirements of FfA and that expectations of the fostering role are made clear in panel training.
- Ensure that panel meeting minutes are robust and reflect the levels of discussion about the applicants' understanding of the FfA role, and that their ability to manage the uncertainties is fully recorded.

Chapter 7
Managing the fostering placement

FfA carers will experience a range of emotions at the beginning of the fostering placement. On the one hand, this is potentially a much longed for child with all of the accompanying excitement, joy and anticipation of an adoption placement, but tempered with the understanding that this is a fostering placement with an outcome that is still uncertain. There is also a need for them to learn about and embrace their new and perhaps previously little thought about role as a local authority or agency foster carer.

It was agreed by all the professionals we spoke to that there must be a clear understanding on the FfA carers' part that their role at this point in time is as a foster carer. This can present challenges for many who will have a hope and an expectation that on completion of proceedings the child will become their adopted child.

As has been discussed in the previous chapter, careful preparation about what the fostering task involves is essential, as well as the need to be clear with FfA carers about the range of uncertainties and risks that are prevalent in the court process. However, whilst they may take on board the training and information offered to them, there will be a further stage of processing that information once the foster placement starts.

The following quotes give a sense of FfA carers' journeys to understanding their fostering role and the differing degrees to which they were able to embrace this.

> *We were dually approved for early permanence when we went to our approval panel. We therefore feel that we were very much adopters through this whole process and were never really intending to be foster carers. In other words, we never once thought, 'Let's do fostering and then hopefully it will turn into adoption'; early permanence to us was one more way of adopting... Before our son was with us, this [the role as a foster carer] was all very much in principle. As such, we didn't feel too much of a weight and, thanks to the training, we did feel like we were prepared for the foster care element. Once he was with us, it all felt very different and I don't think you can stress this difference enough to prospective parents considering this route. Sometimes it felt like decisions were being made in spite of us and it was as though we were*

> *the least important people in the whole situation. When you're caring for a child who you very much see as yours (even with the boundaries you try to set yourself), this can be very unsettling. We were good about talking to each other and keeping each other from getting too bogged down.* (FfA3)
>
> *Our understanding was that there could be a risk but eventually we would be able to adopt; we had certain differences such as who was allowed to visit us, we had contact visits to attend and review meetings. To be completely honest, it was a learning curve as we went along but we were well informed and supported throughout.* (FfA9)
>
> *Being a foster carer was just something that we had to do, so just did it regardless of what we thought about it. We understood why limitations were in place and that these would change if we adopted our little boy so just accepted that's how things are. With regards to family and friends, I don't think they ever viewed us as foster carers. I think they always viewed us as parents, although they all knew that there was a possibility that our little boy could be placed elsewhere.* (FfA2)

It is important that early on in the placement a **foster carer agreement** is completed that will set out expectations of the FfA carers in their role, including the following areas:

- finance arrangements;
- provision of equipment;
- expectation of having household insurance;
- arrangements for supervision and support;
- expectations and provision of training tailored to the FfA role;
- expectations of record keeping;
- annual review and completion of Training and Development Standards (TDS) (see later in this chapter).

An example of a foster carer agreement from Cornwall Council is included in this guide as Appendix 10.

A **placement planning meeting** should also be held, which would include the child's social worker so that the FfA carers are clear about the parameters of their role and of those who are supporting them. This meeting should cover the following areas and result in the placement plan (DfE, 2010, Reg. 9 Schedule 2):

- *purpose and aims of placement;*
- *the child's background;*
- *the child's health and health care needs;*
- *the child's racial, cultural and religious needs;*

- *the child's leisure/recreational needs;*
- *the child's educational needs;*
- *arrangements for financial support;*
- *consent to medical/dental treatment;*
- *the circumstances in which it is necessary to obtain the consent of the responsible authority for the child to live, even temporarily, away from the foster home;*
- *arrangements for visits to the child and the foster home by social workers and other professionals;*
- *the frequency and nature of contact between the child and his/her birth parents and any other significant adults;*
- *arrangements for the LAC review.*

DELEGATED AUTHORITY

Clarity about delegation of authority is a requirement of the placement plan, but given that other professionals may be quite unclear about what an FfA placement involves, it is important that this is established early in placement as FfA carers with young babies are likely to be involved in various meetings with health professionals. Particularly where the FfA carers are first-time parents, these people are an important source of support for them.

It should be made absolutely clear to FfA carers that they cannot change the child's name whilst they are providing a fostering placement and that the child must remain registered under their birth name, for example, at GP surgeries, hospitals, etc. Cornwall Council provides an aide memoire for determining the areas in which an FfA carer can exercise parental responsibility (see the FfA Care Agreement in Appendix 10). As the following quote demonstrates, this can be a frustrating aspect of the role for some FfA carers but clarity about the boundaries is helpful:

> *I found taking him for his injections the most annoying thing because my surgery wouldn't let me give consent and they insisted on verbal consent from someone with parental authority. So I had to get a social worker to speak to the nurse before she would give the jabs. However, arranging this so that there was a social worker available to do it at the time never worked and the admin was so stressful when all we were trying to do was help him!* (CP4)

> *We understood that we were not to leave him with anyone other than the approved carers. There were also things we could not do like get his hair cut, or call ourselves Mum and Dad.* (CP2)

Questions have been raised about the level of information that can be shared with FfA carers whilst they are caring for the child as a foster carer. This issue arises first during the initial matching process but then again during the course of the fostering placement.

PROVISION OF INFORMATION AND CONFIDENTIALITY

The CoramBAAF Practice Note, *The Provision of Information to Fostering for Adoption Carers* (2015) sets out the information required in statutory guidance to be provided to foster carers ahead of a placement:

> *The carer will need to know about the child's family, his/her race, religion and culture, the language spoken at home and any disabilities or other special needs. The carer will generally need to know the circumstances leading to the child becoming looked after, and the child's previous experiences both before and during the care episode. In particular, the carer needs to know what the long-term plan is for the child and its timeframe, what the objectives are for the specific placement being offered and how these fit with the care plan. The carer should be given a copy of the care plan when it is completed and be clear about his/her role in implementing it. Within the context of the care plan, the carer needs a realistic estimate of how long the placement is expected to last.*
>
> (DfE, 2015, s.3.183)

The Practice Note also sets out the need to provide FfA carers with an understanding of their role in safeguarding this information:

> *Training and preparation of Fostering for Adoption carers includes, as part of the discussion of the fostering role, the requirement to maintain confidentiality in respect of information about the child and his/her parents. However, the importance of respecting the confidentiality of the personal information in respect of the child and his/her parents and siblings should be underlined by the inclusion of a confidentiality clause within the fostering agreement.*
>
> (CoramBAAF, 2015)

As one carer in our survey describes:

> *We also had to manage the hopes of our immediate families, and try to explain it to them without disclosing confidential information... We found it hard to manage people's expectations, and got frustrated when people wanted to know more than we could tell them.* (CP3)

SUPPORT

Coram and BAAF (2013) note that the responsibility for the provision of appropriate support must be identified and include regular visits by the child's social worker and the fostering supervising social worker, and access to health and other parenting support services. They highlight that, if an adoption social worker is going to fulfil the role of supervising social worker, they too will need to be familiar with their roles and responsibilities under the fostering regulations.

In our focus groups, there were differences amongst agencies about whether support was offered solely by the FfA carers' adoption social worker, by a fostering social worker or by both. This is further complicated when the FfA carer has been approved as an adopter by a VAA, as unless the agency is also approved as a fostering agency, it is likely that the local authority will want to ensure that the fostering standards are met through supervision by the local authority's adoption or fostering team.

In situations where more than one worker has been identified to provide supervision and support, agencies should be very aware of the need to avoid the carers being overwhelmed by the number of professionals and visits they receive from both social care and health professionals, and the risk of them receiving conflicting information. A number of FfA carers made reference to receiving contradictory advice from different workers or professionals.

> *We had a lot of social worker and health visitor visits and they would often give us contradictory advice – this caused significant stress as you do not want to be proclaimed unfit parents and have your daughter taken off you – I wish that these health professionals would understand the emotional power they have over adoptive parents.* (FfA7)

Striking a balance is not easy – FfA carers are likely to need a higher level of visits than a mainstream foster carer who receives a supervision session every four–six weeks, particularly early in the placement when so much will be new to them, but this needs to be proportionate so that the right people are visiting to offer the support needed by the carers.

> *Additional health appointments were reassuring. It was sometimes disruptive to us and the baby having so many visits from social workers, etc, but it was also good to feel so supported.* (CP3)

We were made aware of a case in which a child care social worker had apparently told FfA carers that they could register the child with their GP and have them known under the prospective adopters' surname. This situation and the example below highlight the importance of training for all the professionals involved so that they are very clear about what FfA means and the limitations of the carers' role at this time.

> *[The child care] social worker thought we had been trained as foster carers rather than simply having attended a one-day course.* (FfA4)

One local authority, where the adoption social worker becomes the fostering social worker in FfA cases, highlighted the challenges posed by the different information being shared by various people, including CAFCASS Guardians and children's social workers who were visiting the child:

> *Information can be disclosed that is unhelpful for our FfA carers to hear and we seek to address this through training so that we can keep a tight grip on these visits, what is being discussed and how it is approached. It is essential to have a common approach in terms of managing expectations, the language used and being mindful about what information should be appropriately shared with FfA carers.* (Local authority worker)

For some FfA carers who had previously adopted, they found the support of their previous child's foster carer invaluable and some agencies have given consideration to the benefits of "buddying" new FfA carers with an adopter who has previously offered FfA or with an experienced foster carer:

> *I had a good level of understanding. I have a close relationship with the foster carer of my older child so she supported me in aspects of foster care that I wasn't previously aware of.* (FfA2)

> *I had a good relationship with the boys' foster carer and she explained a lot to me about contact and the diary and so on. Without her help I would have struggled a lot.* (FfA10)

One local authority had recognised that for first-time parents, having a very young or even newborn baby placed when they had little experience of such a young child could be nerve-wracking and had linked them up with an experienced baby foster carer who could offer practical advice and support. Coram runs baby care training sessions in a group or individually to their concurrent carers, given by a family circle worker.

TRAINING

Many carers will not want or have time to access foster carer training beyond that provided initially about FfA and their role. However, agencies should look at what access to training or support groups they will give to FfA carers and whether they will have any expectations of them in relation to training and the completion of the Training, Support and Development Standards (TSDS) that are appropriate for the FfA role. Statutory Guidance (DfE, 2015a, 3.173) sets out that:

> *The responsible local authority should ensure that they provide appropriate training and development opportunities for these carers so they can carry out their role effectively. Although expected to commence the Training, Support and Development Standards training, it is recognised that the carers might not complete them before the child is placed for adoption with them.*

Agencies should exercise discretion about which sections will be most useful to the FfA carers. Some agencies or consortia have established specific support groups for their concurrent planning or FfA carers, and others have explored giving them access to foster carer training. Gloucestershire County Council ask their FfA carers to complete three courses within their first year of approval as foster carers – Paediatric First Aid, Safeguarding and Infant Care Guidelines. They also give them access to their main training programme and membership of Fostering Network for the period in which they are approved as temporary carers.

FINANCIAL AND PRACTICAL SUPPORT

All FfA carers are entitled to receive the fostering allowance for the period of time that they are fostering the child, and this is set out in Statutory Guidance:

> *Section 22C(9B)(c) placements are foster placements: the carers must be approved foster carers as well as approved prospective adopters before the child can be placed with them. The carers are entitled to the fostering allowances that the fostering provider would normally pay.*

(DfE, 2015a, 3.162)

Some agencies have looked at whether they pay enhanced rates to recognise the level of involvement in contact, etc. Carers should consider whether they need to register as self-employed for the period of time in which they are receiving a fostering allowance; further information is available on the HMRC website at www.hmrc.gov.uk/courses/syob3/fc/HTML/fc_menu.html. In addition, since April 2016, those FfA carers who are eligible to claim statutory adoption pay (SAP) and leave (SAL) can do so at the point of the FfA placement. Further information on this is available at: www.gov.uk/adoption-pay-leave. FfA carers can also look at the options of shared parental leave – further information is available at: www.gov.uk/shared-parental-leave-and-pay. However, this is not always straightforward if the SAP is not immediately claimed at the point of the FfA placement, as this FfA carer found out:

> *I was off work for a year altogether (three months FfA and then nine months adoption leave). The system changed during this time that meant my adoption pay was calculated on my previous three months' salary which, due to the FfA, was nothing! Our social worker had warned*

> *us about this but my employer said it wouldn't be a problem, and my previous salary would be used. However, this wasn't the case and I almost lost a lot of money at the end of my leave. We found the lack of our full income difficult, but luckily we had savings to help us out.* (FfA12)

Most of our respondents had their child placed before 2016 or were not eligible for SAP from the point of placement, but several spoke of receiving the fostering allowance:

> *The financial implications of FfA were the most significant to consider and could have led to us not pursuing this option to adopt. However, our local authority offered us a financial package to support us through the fostering period as there was no pay legislation from employers to support families during that period. As we were the first couple with our local authority to go through FfA, I think that the package that they offered us was generous compared to what they offer as a standard foster payment now that they have put a package in place.* (FfA2)

> *[The main carer] took it [SAP] from the very beginning of the placement. He explained to his employer the nature of the placement and they were happy that it "qualified" as an adoption. The guidance on the local authority and government website could have been much clearer to assist with explaining it to the employer.* (FfA3)

Whilst most families were happy with what they had received, it is important to ensure that FfA carers understand when fostering payments will stop and, if they have decided to stagger receipt of SAP until after the adoption match, that they have information about how this can be achieved and have discussed this with their HR department, where applicable. This has caused some difficulties for local authorities where this was not made clear to their FfA carers, particularly where there was further challenge from the birth parents after the placement was confirmed as an adoption match:

> *Fostering allowances were discussed when our assigned fostering social worker visited... We received the usual fostering allowance... that covered all the baby expenses and some more. This promptly ceased when the placement order was granted. The fostering payments were not expected when we said "yes" to doing a FfA placement; however, they made the whole process sweeter, and therefore when the payments stopped yet the process was still ongoing – it did leave a bitter taste – we had no parental responsibility for the baby, yet all the responsibility!* (FfA1)

Some of our FfA carers had also received some money for equipment, but others did not expect or need this, so while local authorities may have a policy about this, it may also be something that can be discussed with prospective carers on an individual basis:

We received a fostering allowance but we decided not to claim anything back for other expenses. (FfA8)

We had a close friend whose child is slightly older... she also gave us lots of equipment, toys and clothing. (FfA9)

It is also advisable for FfA carers to ensure that their household and car insurance providers are made aware of their fostering role.

CONTACT

Coram and BAAF (2013) highlight that the one principle that must be consistently applied when planning contact arrangements is that the arrangements must protect the child and minimise any exposure they have to undue stress. Research has highlighted the serious issues and adverse consequences when young children are transported to contact in the company of unfamiliar adults, at a contact centre that they do not know, and to meet parents whom they may experience as strangers and with a frequency that has not been set to meet their needs (Kenrick, 2010; Humphreys and Kiraly, 2011). This research also highlighted that the frequency of contact had no bearing on the likelihood of the child being returned to their birth family.

Coram and BAAF (2013) note that in concurrent planning, transporting children to contact is usually undertaken by the carers and they are then available during the contact visit if difficulties arise during contact. However, whether the birth parents meet the carers is something to be decided on a case-by-case basis. The advantages are highlighted:

- it can reassure the birth parents that the carers are caring for the child well, and the carers can actively participate in that by sharing appropriate materials such as diaries, contact books, etc;
- it can help in any subsequent arrangements for contact if the carers go on to adopt the child;
- It can also help the adopters if they have had direct experience of the birth parents to relay that information to the child in the future, where appropriate.

It is also noted that there will be cases where anonymity is the right plan and where this is so, this will impact on any arrangements for contact. However, there may still be a role for the FfA carers in transporting the child, sharing information with the birth parents and being available if the contact does not happen or if the child becomes unduly distressed, but there would need to be careful planning to avoid any risk of the parties meeting. In some instances, the level of risk may lead to a view that an FfA placement is not the right option at this time.

As noted earlier, when FfA was first conceived of it was assumed that FfA carers were less likely to be directly involved in contact arrangements, that they might transport a child to contact but would be unlikely to be involved in the contact meetings. However, as highlighted, the circumstances of the case may lead to a change of expectations or plan. Talking to agencies in our focus groups, we found that a number have an expectation that FfA carers will be involved in transporting the child and in some cases meeting the birth parents.

> *Part of the preparation of FfA carers is to let them know that they will be expected to take the child to and from contact and do a short handover with birth parents at the beginning and end of contact sessions. We explain this in the context of what is best for the baby/child and most FfA carers come to understand this and want to reduce stress to the child rather than do what they feel might be best for them as adults. For all the reasons that are present in concurrent planning cases (less stress for the child when travelling in a familiar car with familiar carers, a relationship developing between parents and carers, the likelihood of a more coherent narrative for children from their carers post-adoption), we feel it is of the same importance for children placed in an FfA arrangement...*
>
> *My experience from training FfA carers is that once prospective FfA carers understand the reasons – that the procedure is designed ultimately to benefit the child – they usually fully embrace it. It can of course raise some initial anxiety for both birth parents and FfA carers but careful management and social work support can alleviate this. All the cases that I have been involved in where FfA carers have transported the baby/child and met birth parents at contact sessions have been emotionally successful for all concerned and the child's experience of contact has presumably been better than it would have been if a "stranger" had collected and transported him/her. We have of course had some cases where this approach has not been suitable, mainly due to serious threats from birth parents. I feel, however, that this should be the exception rather than the norm and only be resorted to when there is a very real threat/dangerous situation from the birth parents.*
>
> (Local authority social worker)

It was clear that individual circumstances meant that differing arrangements were being made to respond to the situations that arose.

There was evidence of potentially negative impact on young children and babies from contact arrangements from the information we gathered from agencies, where we heard of situations where children had become distressed by their experiences of contact. One local authority shared details of a baby going to contact three times a week where the FfA carers noticed that the baby was distressed on returning from contact. Specifically, on one occasion the baby was not focusing and had no eye movement at all. Following examination, it transpired that there was no physical problem with the eye function, but that the child was experiencing a negative emotional response to contact and was effectively "shutting down".

Some of the FfA carers also reported a negative impact on their children from contact:

> *Contact was one-and-a-half hours, three mornings a week and was arranged fairly locally... Contact was sporadic and he was quite distressed at times after it. The birth parents smoked and he was hyper-sensitive to smell at that time. We often had to change his clothes before bringing him home and sometimes even had to wash him just to calm him down again. Due to the sporadic nature of the birth parents' attendance at contact, as he grew older and more aware of his surroundings, he was less happy at being left with strangers.* (FfA8)

> *Once our little boy came to us, I had to take him to contact three times a week with his birth mother and once a week with his birth father. (His father's contact followed on from his mothers'.) This involved 30–45 minute journeys each time. Our little man was shattered when he returned and we just had to sit and cuddle for ages afterwards. I believe all this passing around was hard for a little baby.* (FfA12)

These examples graphically demonstrate the importance of ensuring that contact plans are focused around the needs of the child and reviewed where it is evident that they are not meeting the child's needs, and that the contact plan is changed where needed.

In several examples, we heard of relatives who had come forward during care proceedings where some degree of contact had to be introduced to aid assessments, and there were a small number of examples where the circumstances of the case changed and the baby was eventually returned to the birth parents. This means that FfA carers may at times be asked to be involved in contact arrangements that they had not anticipated or been prepared for, and highlights the importance of covering all possible scenarios and outcomes with them during their preparation for placement.

Feedback from our FfA carers and concurrent carers also demonstrated the range of experiences that they found themselves dealing with and the impact on them and on the child:

> *The contact visits involved me handing over our son to a social worker in a car park, which always felt so sad for him, being passed around. On one occasion, when I was taking him to contact with his birth mother, no one came to collect him. In the end, I had to take him into the contact centre and his birth mother saw him. We initially felt anxious about this, but as we were later able to meet her anyway, it didn't matter. For safety*

> *reasons, there was always a time delay to avoid us coming into contact with birth parents.* (FfA12)
>
> *We found the contact meetings really difficult, mainly being without him, so it was arranged for me to attend alongside the contact worker for the traveling to and from prison.* (FfA9)
>
> *He had contact three days a week to start with and at first that was OK as I expected it and it was in the plan, but it got harder when the birth parents didn't turn up or the baby came home having not been fed.* (FfA10)

The concurrent carers who contacted us had been more directly involved in contact arrangements:

> *We met with her early on and she seemed happy with us and pleased we were going to look after him. Informally we discussed it at contact. Some of our contact took place in a drug rehabilitation unit, where we stayed because there was nowhere locally to go so I spent quite some time with her. When we eventually adopted him she gave us her blessing. We genuinely liked each other.* (CP2)
>
> *[The birth father] is very violent so when he showed up (for contact) when he wasn't supposed to, the social workers were very quick to remove him and to keep my son and me safe. However, it did feel scary at the time... During contact the birth mother and I did chat. Our son got so distressed in contact that no one could settle him so I stayed in most contact sessions with her and the contact supervisor.* (CP4)

The feelings invoked for FfA carers involved in contact will be very different to those of short-term foster carers due to the additional emotional investment for them in the child. The following examples demonstrate the importance of providing support to the carers that recognises these emotions, whilst helping them to see this as part of their fostering role:

> *We had a contact planning meeting and then had contact once per week with the birth mother only. This was done via social services as the birth mother did not want to meet us in person at this point. We met in a car park and handed over our son, then collected him an hour or two later... Contact proved difficult, as the birth mother did not engage every week. We had to be on standby each week and sometimes only got a confirmation that it was happening that morning. Equally at the times she did show up, it meant having to pass the child we saw as our own to someone else. This was another example of "being OK in principle, but something quite different in practice". We did not expect his birth mother to dress him in girls' clothing and were really surprised that many of the clothes she sent for us to dress him in were of very poor quality, and some were even soiled. We had no choice other than to comply though, which felt like we were doing the "wrong" thing (i.e. something we*

> *wouldn't ordinarily do). That said, I am pleased we made the effort and rode the wave of contact, as we will be able to tell our son that we did this and made all efforts we possibly could to make his contact sessions a success.* (FfA3)

The following account is from an FfA carer who had to support the child placed with her in a return to his birth parents:

> *He had contact three times a week at a place about 45 mins away – he was picked up by a contact supervisor. When he was about to go back into the [residential] unit as part of a rehabilitation plan, that contact took place at the unit which was an hour-and-a-half away, and I drove him up there, and the contact supervisor drove him back... It was essentially very hard to establish routines, as the journey and the fact he would have a bottle at contact meant he slept at funny times, plus was often left to sleep for most of contact, so we then had some pretty sleepless nights off the back of him sleeping for whole afternoons! The trips to the unit were awful, he often cried for a large part of the journey and more than once I was told he'd cried most of the way home by contact supervisors.*
>
> *Dealing with contact supervisors was one of the most difficult things day by day, as at least two were not very professional and asked questions/ made comments that were inappropriate. I found dealing with the unit much better, they were very professional. He was a very lovely baby so it was hard to see him being disrupted a lot by the journeys and feeling it was causing a lot of strain for him. I was glad to meet the birth parents and found that helpful in having a fostering view of the situation.* (FfA4)

This example highlights the benefits of a consistent and well trained contact supervisor.

SECURITY AND CONFIDENTIALITY

Issues of security and confidentiality are key considerations when arranging and managing contact for children placed with FfA carers, as can be demonstrated by the following examples below. Social workers need to ensure that names and addresses are kept confidential in any paperwork but also to think ahead when planning how situations should be managed when FfA carers and birth parents are both involved, for example, at contact or LAC review meetings:

> *We had met the birth parents when adopting [our first child] and we were told they were happy the boys were together. They said if [the second child] was adopted, they wanted him to come to us. Because he was already with us, there were issues with contact – making sure our address and names weren't on information passed to the birth parents and making sure meetings were separate.* (FfA10)

Whilst adoption social workers may be more aware of the need to protect the FfA carers' identity, other professionals, such as contact supervisors or IROs, who are more used to dealing with children in mainstream fostering placements, may need to be reminded of the importance of ensuring confidentiality. This is a particular consideration in those arenas where there is more likely to be unplanned contact between the birth parents and FfA carers, or where written information is being shared, such as by children's social workers or local authority legal teams and their administrators in court.

> *The local authority gave away details of our occupations and address to the birth family, with very serious ramifications. We have since moved house and are now registered anonymously on the electoral roll. Safety and security continue to be issues and no one in our family has any social media presence at all – which has caused serious professional difficulties.* (CP1)

> *LAC reviews were a little awkward because the birth parents couldn't be present as we had him in our care, and so there was one time we were ushered out the back door and down some alleyway as the birth mum was out the front! He was too young to feel the impact of any of this though.* (FfA10)

> *I had to attend the LAC review without any social worker support for me, and met the birth father (whom I knew to have violent tendencies) outside the meeting, completely unaccompanied, which was not ideal!* (FfA4)

WHEN THERE IS A CHALLENGE TO THE LOCAL AUTHORITY PLAN OR THE CHILD RETURNS TO THEIR BIRTH FAMILY

Prospective adopters entering into an FfA placement will inevitably be hoping that the child remains with them and adoption is the final outcome, but previous experience from concurrent planning projects tells us that there will be a small number of cases where the child will be returned to the care of either a birth parent or family member. FfA carers may have been told that the local authority has reached the view that adoption should be the plan for the child, but must also be aware that there can be changes or challenges that emerge during the FfA placement. Where circumstances then change following the FfA placement being made, FfA carers will need significant support to manage changing contact arrangements where further assessments are then ordered by the court for birth parents or family members, and particularly if the care plan then changes to support the child's return to their birth family.

During our focus groups, we were made aware of several such situations that had developed.

In one case, a newborn baby had been placed with FfA carers for six months when an aunt came forward for an assessment for a special guardianship order that led to an order being granted. The impact on the prospective adopters was significant although, in this case, they were able to maintain ongoing contact with the baby within the special guardianship placement and this was seen as positive by all parties in maintaining attachments for the child.

In another case involving a baby placed under FfA, there were protracted court proceedings in what initially was considered to be a robust case for adoption; however, during proceedings, the birth mother had started a relationship with a new partner who subsequently applied to be assessed for a special guardianship order. The FfA carers brought in their own legal team and were made party to proceedings. The child was returned to the care of her birth mother and her new partner for a further period of assessment before the final order was made, but the FfA carers' legal team successfully argued that the FfA carers should have ongoing contact, at least until the final order, as they had established a significant relationship with the baby. However, it would be unusual for FfA carers to be made party to proceedings.

In a further case, a baby was placed directly from hospital and shorty after there was a viability assessment carried out on a birth grandfather, which was negative. A further viability assessment proved more positive and the final full assessment on the grandfather recommended a special guardianship order, even though many professionals had some serious concerns about the viability of the placement. The FfA carers were devastated at having to hand over the child.

Yet another case was cited where the child was with FfA carers for 10 months and the birth grandparents applied to be assessed to care for the child. The grandparents found it difficult to work with the FfA carers, who needed to take time out and needed lots of support from their worker, but the final outcome was that the assessment was not positive and the child went on to be adopted.

The key issue in such cases will be the provision of support to the FfA carers and their family members throughout, and ensuring that all the professionals involved are aware of the psychological and emotional impact on the carers during a heightened period of uncertainty, or where the child is to be returned at a time of significant loss for them and to be sensitive to their circumstances.

Borthwick and Donnelly (2013) highlighted that in these cases, concurrent carers and birth parents need a very intense level of support and that it is essential that workers' time is available to the carers. The same will apply for FfA carers experiencing such situations.

> *Those workers who have been involved with the carers and parents during the assessment phase are often best placed to offer this support, although independent counselling may also be offered. Workers will need to continue to be present for every handover and contact between carer and parents. This gives the message that no party is alone and everyone remains clear about the plan and what is going to happen. Workers need to be available at any time over the reunification period and the out of hours service for foster carers should be alerted to the potential need to provide additional contact and support to the carers, as required. Rehabilitations through concurrency can be isolating for concurrent carers who may feel set apart from other carers who have gone on to adopt their children.*
>
> (Borthwick and Donnelly, 2013)

In particular, there should be an awareness of the need to support the FfA carers in enabling a positive transition for the child whilst managing their own feelings.

After the placement has ended, agencies have also looked at holding a professionals' meeting or indeed a review meeting, which in some cases the FfA carers have wanted to attend, so that the agency can learn lessons from what has happened and the FfA carers can be supported with their grieving and healing process.

The FfA carers will also need to be supported, at the right time for them, in thinking about their future plans to adopt. Some carers have chosen to take a second FfA placement; others choose to return to the "traditional" route; and for some they may feel, at least at this time, that they do not wish to pursue a further placement.

We received feedback from an FfA carer who was involved in returning her first child through FfA to their birth parent, but then went on to have a second FfA placement that led to adoption. The following extracts from her account help to show how she and her family managed this experience and were able to move on to adopt again through FfA.

> *We were attracted to FfA because we feel it really does serve the needs of the child by limiting change where possible, and having two adopted children already made us see the value of that. Essentially, we felt that we could do it and it was a good thing, so we decided to do it! Whilst you need to be utterly committed to the child, and excited about the possibility of adopting, you also need to be fully aware of the rights of both birth parents and children, and the court's ultimate role in decision making. You need to be wanting the best for the child even if the best is not being with you, as however great adoption is, it does have a huge impact for the child and can't be taken lightly.*
>
> *During the residential assessment, there was a long and slow period of uncertainty and of gradually letting go of him; I felt I processed a lot of*

grief (driving up and down to the unit for contact in the last two weeks) and meeting his birth parents was really helpful in preventing me from making up a narrative where someone had taken "our" baby away.

We loved him deeply, he was a gorgeous little boy and we didn't hold back from him in terms of love and affection, but he was, is, their baby and not ours. We will always have him in our hearts, and we have photos of him around here and there, but it was important to grasp that for his birth parents this was a chance they had fought for, and we needed to try and want for it to now work out for everyone's sake.

Over the summer after he left, my husband and I did fairly standard grieving with all that involves, periods of anger, feeling numb, etc. But by the October, when we sat down with the social workers to talk about where we were up to after the final hearing, we felt we were no longer raw in our grief. We also felt confident that the girls were in a good emotional state, and all of us felt we had it in us to try again. I also felt I knew that we would be fine if we didn't get another placement, which is what I had felt before we embarked on being assessed for the second time – I did not feel that we had a hole that had to be filled, which made me confident that we were not trying to "replace" him or bury that grief in that way.

In lots of ways, experiencing the "worst case scenario", as I guess most prospective FfA adopters would see it, meant we knew the worst that could happen and that we could weather it. And more than that, we felt passionately that FfA is great for the child, and wanted to do it for that reason as well. Ultimately, he experienced eight weeks of devoted, attuned, loving, excellent family life, and that will mean something for his future development. (FfA4)

Chapter 8
Progressing the adoption match

MATCHING CONSIDERATIONS

Once the placement order has been made, the match for adoption can then be agreed and taken to the adoption panel. The planning for this can start prior to the order being made, but it is important to recognise the significance of this event for FfA carers and give them some time to process their relief and excitement that they can now "claim the child as their own", as they move towards this becoming an adoption placement. It should also be recognised that in some cases they may be feeling some sadness for the birth parents and their situation. This will be a life-changing decision for the FfA family and they should have some time to reflect and confirm they are ready to move to becoming the child's adoptive family.

> *One of the hardest things was knowing that for him to stay and become a member of our family, another set of parents had to lose him. This broke my heart. I found it hard to reconcile my desperate desire to keep him with the fact that for this to happen, someone had to lose him.* (FfA12)

Although the agency will have already considered the appropriateness of the match before making the FfA placement, there should still be a formal consideration of the match so that the adoption placement report can be prepared for the panel. Social workers will be able to consider the relationships that have already developed between the prospective adopters, their family and the child, and will have evidence of the care they have provided during the time of the fostering placement. There will also be evidence of how they have managed the changes to their lifestyle and family situation, particularly if there are other children in the family.

This stage of planning should also be used by workers to reflect and focus on the long-term strengths of the family and the possible challenges going forward. Social workers should allow space for the adopters to reflect on whether they have any concerns that they need to raise at this time and to discuss their short-term and longer term support needs.

There may have been new information shared during care proceedings and it will be important for the adoption medical to be updated where needed. It will also be important for the prospective adopters to be given the opportunity to meet with a medical adviser if this did not happen before placement or if significant new information has emerged, so that they have an opportunity to think and talk through the longer term implications of the birth family's and child's health history.

Agencies should also consider whether a "life appreciation day" would be beneficial. Life appreciation days can offer important opportunities to capture information from a range of people involved with the birth parents and in the child's early life. One agency reported that about 50 per cent of their FfA carers had wanted to take up this opportunity, whilst others felt that there were no gaps in their knowledge as they had been the child's foster carers from such an early stage.

FfA carers we heard from also confirmed that they had 'known the child from birth' or 'knew the family history as they already had an older sibling'. Nevertheless, some noted the lack of information that they had at the time of the adoption match, particularly information about birth family members and health histories:

> *As we had [our child] pretty much from birth, we thought that we had most information at that point. It was only at his two-year review that we found out from the hospital staff that he was the worst drug case they'd had and they thought he would either die or be a very damaged child. It was at that appointment they signed him off and said he was in perfect health, meeting all his milestones and they didn't feel they needed to see him again.* (FfA8)

> *As she was only just born, we had only bits of information about birth family – and insufficient medical information on the birth father, which we struggled for years to access.* (CP1)

> *I don't think we had all the information about our son by the time we got to panel. We learned new stuff from his life story book!* (CP4)

When writing the Adoption Placement Report (APR), there should be updated information provided on the adoptive family since their approval, which can include information about their experience of caring for the child. The CoramBAAF APR provides a section for an up-to-date profile of the prospective adopter/s where this information can be recorded.

The views of the birth family must be considered and recorded when preparing the APR. As reported by agencies and some of the FfA carers we heard from, it is not uncommon for birth parents to feel more positive about the adoption plan, knowing that the child will be staying with their current carers, and sometimes as a result of having met the FfA carers through contact or other meetings.

> *The birth parents requested a meeting with us to tell us they no longer opposed the adoption and they gave us their "blessing" to adopt her.* (FfA1)
>
> *The very last time we saw the birth mother, it was the week of Mother's Day, so we had flowers to give to her and she said that if he had to be adopted, she wanted it to be us, otherwise she would fight it.* (FfA8)

The APR will also include the Adoption Support Plan, as required by Adoption Agencies Reg. 31 (DfE, 2013a), and although many of the children in FfA placements will be very young, it will be important that the Support Plan highlights any possible longer term implications, for example, as a result of pre-birth exposure to alcohol or drugs, as well as the birth parents' health histories, so prospective adopters are aware that they can access support services in future years. It was a concern for us that very few of the FfA or concurrent planning carers who responded to us showed much awareness of their entitlements to future support services.

THE ROLE OF THE MATCHING PANEL

Coram and BAAF (2013) highlight that adoption panels still have an important role to play when considering the match of a child placed in an FfA placement once the placement order is made, and that they need to be prepared and briefed for their role. They recognise that, in considering an adoption match when the child and carers have already developed a significant relationship, the panel will have the advantage of direct evidence of the quality of that placement from prepared reports, but note that its role is still to make a recommendation about a placement that is fundamentally changing its legal and psychosocial status from foster care to adoption. In that sense, they see the role of the panel as not to "rubber stamp" that which has already happened, but to openly and supportively explore what has happened and what might need to happen.

The role of the adoption panel, when considering whether to recommend the adoption match of a child who is already placed with their carers, is one that panel members will already be familiar with, from considering matches of foster carers applying to adopt a child in their care. They will therefore be aware that, whilst the placement is (presumably) currently working well, it is essential that the long-term issues for the child and family are fully explored and the panel is satisfied that they can offer a robust permanent adoptive placement throughout the child's life to adulthood.

In the case of a foster carer adopting, the placement will not have been made with adoption seen as the likely outcome and the carers will not have been assessed to adopt. However, in the case of an FfA carer being considered as suitable to adopt the child in their care, the carers will already have been approved as prospective adopters and it would be expected that there would already have been careful consideration of many of the issues pertinent to an adoption match at the point of placement with the carers.

Although a couple of the FfA carers we heard from talked about seeing the panel as a "for the sake of it" exercise or "another tick in the right box", it is nevertheless important that social workers and the prospective adopters understand that the panel is not a "rubber stamp" exercise. Although there would need to be significant concerns and evidence to support any panel recommendation that the match should not proceed, we were made aware of one situation in which an adoption panel had deferred making their recommendation as they were not satisfied that the adoption support plan had been fully thought through.

There are some key questions that should be addressed at the adoption panel considering the match, partly to inform the panel recommendation but also to fulfill the quality assurance aspect of the panel's role:

- What has been the prospective adopters' experience of caring for the child and what have they learned about the child during the time that they have been caring for him or her? Have there been challenges or things they had not expected and how have they dealt with them?
- Have the prospective adopters received all the known information about the child *at the point of this match* and had an opportunity to consider this with their adoption social worker and with the agency medical adviser, so that they are aware of all the known and unknown future implications for them in parenting the child?
- Is there a clear assessment of the child's needs and the prospective adopters' ability to meet those needs, both in the short and longer term?
- Do they have a good understanding of the support that will be available to them in the short and longer term from the placing authority and, where different, from their approving agency, and are they confident about being able to access that support? (Where they live outside of the local authority area, this will include knowing how to access support from their own local authority once three years have passed since the adoption order.)
- What are the birth parents' views and have they been given information about/accessed independent birth parent counselling? How will they be helped to engage in future letterbox arrangements?
- Have the contact arrangements been clearly set out and agreed? (This should include any sibling contact that may not have been considered appropriate during the FfA placement but is in the children's best interest in the long term.)

ATTENDANCE AT PANEL

There can be practical issues to consider when prospective adopters are attending the panel about whether the child can be brought to the venue of the panel meeting/is able to come into the meeting, with differing views being held about this.

For some prospective adopters, including a number of the FfA carers we heard from, this will not be an issue and they will make arrangements with family members or friends known to the child to care for them, either at home or outside the panel meeting. In some cases, we heard that social workers or contact supervisors who knew the child sat with the child outside the panel meeting. However, other FfA carers have been reluctant to leave the child with other people or were concerned about the impact of that separation.

The concerns expressed by panel Chairs and panel members are about the impact of having a baby in the meeting, which can be both disruptive and distracting for the adopters as well as for panel members.

These issues should be considered before the panel meeting, with the Chair being included in any discussions about agreeing a general policy, or in individual cases where it is felt an exception is needed.

The following accounts from FfA carers set out how they managed this issue and overall how they found the panel experience:

> *[Our son] was cared for by my parents. We were the first couple to go through the process in our local authority so they asked us about how this experience had compared to adoption down the traditional route. They also wanted to know what we had told our two children about the possibility that he wouldn't remain with us and how we had prepared everyone for that eventuality. We felt the questions were relevant to our situation.* (FfA2)

> *I took our son to panel and the contact supervisor came on work experience, and she was going to look after him while I went into the panel. But fortunately the Chair of the panel let him come in too! That was a huge relief because he got very distressed at that time about being separated from me. I think it was good for the panel to see the real child they were making decisions about.* (CP4)

> *We felt that as FfA was so new, the matching panel hadn't been adapted to keep up with the changes. Having been expected to keep our son close to us all the time from when he first moved in, we had never left him even for a moment with anyone else (apart from at contact). Suddenly, we were expected to leave him with someone whilst we met the panel! ... A lot of the questions were completely irrelevant as they were of the kind, 'How do you think you will ...' when we were clearly already doing these things. We already knew how our daughter would be with*

> *him as he already lived with us! It was a relaxed environment but didn't feel particularly relevant. We were obviously relieved once it was over as it was a step closer to him becoming our son forever. One lovely moment was that the panel asked us to bring him into the room after the questions, which was really nice.* (FfA12)

As this example demonstrates, it is important that the panel's questions recognise the lived experience that FfA carers will already have had with the child, as well as then looking forward to the longer term issues.

Where babies are brought to the venue/panel meeting, it can be used as a positive occasion to mark the significant change in the status of the placement, and one agency told us of adopters who asked the panel to pose for a photo with the child for their life story work.

Once the adoption decision-maker decision has been made, the placement will then become an adoption placement – for some prospective adopters, this may just be a confirmation of what they already feel, but for others it can feel like a very significant step in their journey to become an adoptive family.

> *Once approval was granted it was wonderful. The girls were thrilled, as were family and friends. It was great to just get on with normal life not having a cloud of uncertainty hanging over us.* (FfA10)

> *It was a great feeling – it was a little surreal as we'd had him since birth and viewed him as ours by this point. But we were very excited that it was moving on.* (FfA8)

> *Once the match was agreed and the placement was recognised as an adoptive placement, we were thrilled but very sad for [our child's] birth mother. However, by this time she knew it was the right thing and had given us her blessing. It was quite hard to hold all that sad information about her life and [our child's] alternative life for all that time and this moment felt like the beginning of a new life for all of us.* (CP2)

Chapter 9
Post-match considerations and adoption support

BECOMING AN ADOPTION PLACEMENT

Once the match is agreed by the decision-maker, the placement will be recognised as an adoptive placement. There are legal requirements that then need to be followed, which were developed to support adoptive families but which may at times feel less helpful for adopters who have already been living with their child/ren for some time. We heard from agencies about how they manage some of these issues.

The agency is still required to hold a planning meeting (DfE, 2013a, s.5.3) and an Adoption Placement Plan must be prepared, as although the child is already in placement there will still be issues to be discussed and agreed.

The following issues (as set out in DfE, 2013a, Schedule 5) will still be relevant:

(a) To agree the date when the child became placed for adoption with the prospective adopter.

This will be particularly relevant if the adopters are starting their Statutory Adoption Pay and Leave from this date and will also be the date when fostering payments would cease.

(b) Notifications of the adoptive placement to other agencies – health, education and the local authority where the family lives.

(c) The arrangements for statutory visits and review of the placement.

The timescales for statutory visits set out in DfE, 2013a, 36(3), namely within one week of the placement and then at least once a week until the first review, may feel excessive to the family, who will be readjusting to family life without the demands of a fostering placement, so this needs to be thought about so the family and the child's needs are met.

One option we heard about from a local authority is that they will hold the first review after placement earlier than four weeks so that social workers can then agree at the review what level of visits are needed if it is felt that weekly visits are not necessary.

(d) *The agreements for parental responsibility of the prospective adopter for the child and how it is to be restricted.*

Agreements about the exercise of delegated authority that were in place while the prospective adopters were providing a fostering placement can now be reviewed, as the placement is now an adoptive placement.

(e) *The provision of adoption support services for the adoptive family and the child.*

(f) *The agreed contact arrangements and how these will be facilitated and supported.*

Plans for a gradual reduction in existing contact arrangements, leading to a "final" or "wish you well" contact meeting, should be realistic in what both the birth parents and the child can manage and should not be protracted once the plan for adoption has been agreed.

The plans for post-adoption contact should be based on an assessment of the child's ongoing needs and for most young children are likely to involve indirect contact arrangements. However, we were made aware of situations where, due to the FfA carers' involvement in contact arrangements while the child was in foster care, there were occasions during the court process when CAFCASS Guardians or others requested consideration of continuing direct contact that placed FfA carers in a difficult situation, and in some where the final care plan was changed to include direct contact. These situations need to be dealt with by the social workers so FfA carers are not placed under pressure to agree to something that they had not expected to be considering, and where necessary the local authority should be prepared to withstand pressure to amend their care plan when they do not believe direct contact is in the child's best interests. If a local authority finds itself in this situation, they would be advised to ensure that a review of contact arrangements is included after the first year.

(g) *The dates when the child's life story book and later life letter are to be passed by the adoption agency to the prospective adopter.*

(h) *Any other arrangements that need to be made.*

At the first review following adoption placement (within four weeks of the date on which the child is placed for adoption), a discussion can be held about when the adoption application should be made. The child will probably have been living with the adopters for a number of weeks or months by this time and once the child has been in a continuous placement with them for 10 weeks, whether as a fostered child or placed for adoption, the prospective adopters are able to lodge their application with the court with agreement from the LAC review.

Prospective adopters need to be prepared for the possibilities of further challenge by the birth parents during the application for an adoption order. Whilst they may have prepared well for the uncertainties of the fostering period, they need to understand that increasing challenges to the adoption order are being allowed by courts and may create further delay in the final order being made.

However, where older children have been placed, it will be important for the timing to take account of their wishes and feelings. They may still be adjusting to reducing contact arrangements and need time to come to terms with final contacts before they are ready to make a commitment to the adoptive family and embrace their adoptive status. This may be a period when further direct work is needed.

Further reviews must take place not more than three months after the first review, and then every six months till the adoption order is made.

ADOPTION SUPPORT

Many of the FfA carers who responded to us saw their family and friends as their primary source of support, as well as other adoptive parents with whom they were in contact.

> *We are very proactive about our support network. We rely on family for emotional needs and then our network of long-time friends is there for us as well. We are good at making friends in the adoption world and then in the local community at baby groups, etc. It has been a godsend to have people we can talk to and lean on in all these circles. If you keep yourself closed off, this route to starting a family could be very stressful.* (FfA3)

In addition, most of the children who are being placed in FfA arrangements are young, often under a year old. Whilst some of the FfA carers were aware or satisfied with the support they received, for others they were seemingly unaware of their entitlement to an assessment of their adoption support needs.

Whilst in the short term many of them were not expecting to need adoption support services, for the concurrent planning carers who had adopted their children a few years before, there was more of a growing awareness that their children might need adoption support services, but sometimes a lack of clarity about their entitlement to them or how to access them.

> *I did not know that we were entitled to an assessment of our support needs. In fact, as I write that, I'm surprised to hear it was an option – was it available four years ago? If so, we had no idea! I would have liked to have known. I think it would have helped and been very useful for all of us.* (CP4)

> *We now feel that the contact arrangements might have had a detrimental effect on [our son] and left him with some attachment anxiety that exhibits itself in anger from time to time. We might need some support for this.* (CP2)

> *We were told about an adoption allowance we would get as the boys were siblings and this was agreed, but there was a mess-up and it took a while to kick in. We were not told about an assessment of needs as such; we had to move to a bigger house and buy a bigger car. [The local authority] did pay for the removal company but nothing else.* (FfA10)

It is important that the adoption support plans developed at the point of a match are revised during reviews following placement and are understood by prospective adopters to be a source of information about where they can go if future support needs arise for them or their child. They should be given a copy of the Adoption Passport that sets out their entitlements to early education for children from the age of two, the Early Years Pupil Premium for three and four-year-olds, the Pupil Premium Plus, and priority access to school places. Support in education for previously looked after children will be strengthened when the Children and Social Work Act 2017 is implemented, in 2018. They should also be made aware of the provisions of the Adoption Support Fund (ASF) (www.adoptionsupportfund.co.uk).

Applications to the ASF can be made for interventions that will start once the child is placed and prior to the adoption order being made, so early identification and planning are important. For older children, there may be identified needs such as therapeutic life story work or other interventions to help them work through feelings about their past.

It is important that child care social workers are aware of the future implications of some of the experiences children have had, often pre-birth, so adopters are not left unaware of what can be on offer, or left with the message given to one of the FfA carers who responded to us:

> *We were advised that we wouldn't get any support as the child does not have any special needs at this stage.* (FfA6)

> *I do feel that once the adoption is granted, you are on your own! When people have children of their own there is support in the way of the National Childbirth Trust, e.g. classes, and lots of good things to help. But I often felt that once the adoption order was done you were left, unless of course you have adopted a child with complex issues and support systems are in place.* (FfA5)

As with all adopters, it is helpful for the adoption or adoption support team to keep a link with FfA adopters post-placement and post-adoption so that, if they want to, they can involve themselves in support groups, training events or social activities, or just keep an awareness of services through a newsletter so that they know how to access support if necessary.

In an outcomes study (Coram, 2013) on 57 children placed through Coram for concurrent planning between 2000 and 2011, 28 families were interviewed about their experiences and this study provides some useful indicators for adoption services about the future support needs of families adopting young children through early permanence routes such as concurrent planning or FfA.

The main services used by these families were those from their approving agency's (Coram) adoption support services (64%), services through CAMHS (36%), their local authority's support services (32%), and other adoptive parents (32%). In addition to advice and support by both phone or through home visits, they valued seminars, workshops and parenting programmes. They sought support on life story work, contact issues and parenting skills and had attended training on topics such as education, internet safety, and identity. One-third of the families had accessed therapeutic services through CAMHS or other therapeutic services and three families had received financial support from the responsible local authority.

The other main area in which these families had needed support was from schools – some had found their schools helpful but others reported experiencing significant challenges.

As we heard from some of the concurrent planning carers who responded to us, some adopters expressed uncertainty about 'knowing who to ask for help and what is available, and where can they access it... and did not know who they should contact for post-adoption support.' Where they were not living in the area in which the child had been placed or had moved out of the area, they would have liked to have been linked into and had greater access to services in their present local area.

This study highlighted that adopters who have adopted young children through concurrent planning or FfA are still likely to have some support needs, with about one-third of families managing children with more significant needs, many of which had not been apparent/identified at the time of placement. When preparing adoption support plans and talking to adopters about their future needs, it is therefore important that they are given a positive message about the likelihood of them needing to access support services and clear information about how to access that support.

ADOPTION SUPPORT FOR CONTACT

The other area in which support arrangements need to be clearly set out and available is around post-adoption contact, both direct and indirect. Whilst some of the issues for adopters who have offered FfA or concurrent planning placements will be similar to those for other adopters, they are more likely to have previous knowledge and sometimes a relationship with the birth parents that will mean they may need help with both the practical and emotional issues that arise. In his book on planning for contact, Adams (2012, p 19) notes that in her research Beth Neil suggests:

> *There are many real obstacles with indirect contact that can adversely impact on the quality of information exchange. These obstacles can include difficulties within the agency acting as a third party such as delays, etc, but are mainly to do with the difficulty of communicating in writing where birth relatives and permanent carers may struggle to know exactly what to say; where correspondence crosses in the post so questions do not get answered; and where children, especially babies and toddlers, can be excluded from the process. Some adoptive parents do not like to write too fully as it might sound like they are boasting about their lives, and some birth relatives do not have the skills or confidence to convey what they really want to say, and may receive variable support from the agency.*

These themes were also seen in some of the experiences of the FfA carers we heard from; several had letterbox arrangements that were only one way, and whilst some were happy with the arrangements and support in place, others seemed less clear about the support available.

> *We have once a year letterbox contact with the birth mum and siblings that we have never found satisfactory. The tone and content have been inappropriate and our daughter found it disturbing. We are now trying to reduce the contact and have been having support from (our agency) to do this.* (CP1)

> *[We have] annual letterbox letter for birth parents... Letterbox contact hasn't been great because we didn't have a contact agreement and had no idea whether our letters had been received by the local authority, let alone by the birth parents.* (CP3)

> *We are supposed to receive three letters a year via letterbox contact, but we have only had one letter in four years. I suspect the birth mum is so vulnerable that it is hard for her to get things together to write and also to cope with the emotional implications of keeping in touch with a birth child who has been adopted. I always worry that when our letters are forwarded to the birth mum and birth dad, they don't prompt him to return to her. He was so violent towards her. It worries me that our contact might restart the cycle. I hate living with that thought and I really hope social services are sensitive to that issue but I doubt they are! It's not pleasant to live with.* (CP4)

We also heard about direct contact arrangements and some of the anxieties and difficulties that had arisen for adopters. These examples also highlight the importance of adopters knowing where they can access support, particularly where agreed contact has not been sustained or when it becomes stressful or difficult.

> *[We have] direct contact with maternal half-siblings four times a year... Mutually agreed between us and our child's social worker.*
>
> *(Are you satisfied with the support you have received with contact arrangements?)*
>
> *No, we were only provided a leaflet. We would have liked a social worker to visit to discuss fully what will happen and what we need to do.* (FfA6)
>
> *We receive letters through a letterbox service annually. The birth father has never contacted us using this service; the birth mum has contacted three times and seems to be keeping this up in recent years. We are supposed to see a half-sibling annually who is also adopted. We have met once when we just had our adopted daughter before our son was born. The half-sister has global developmental delay. Although we met up with the adoptive family, we got the impression that they didn't think it would help their daughter to remain in contact as she didn't understand who we were and why we were meeting. Whilst the family by no means said this, it is just a feeling that we got, and when we have tried to engage with them since, they have not responded. We have therefore not had any contact with them in about three years.* (FfA2)

Conclusion

Fostering for Adoption was introduced in 2013 as a route to achieving an early placement for children who are unlikely to be able to be cared for in their birth family. By placing them with prospective adopters who are also approved as foster carers, it was intended that this family would be able to offer the child security of placement during the course of care proceedings and the decision making about whether adoption is the right plan. The introduction of section 22c(9) of the 1989 Children Act means that the consideration of an early permanence placement is not optional but a requirement as part of the local authority permanence planning process for children where adoption is being considered.

It is evident from our enquiries that local authorities, VAAs and, going forward, RAAs, see FfA as an important route to achieving early permanence alongside concurrent planning, and whilst they are at varying stages of embedding the practice into their agencies, we were encouraged to hear about the progress that is being made.

However, it is also clear that as the use of FfA placements has increased using both temporary approval and dual approval, there is evidence of a continuum of early permanence placements developing. We have heard examples of FfA families finding themselves managing situations of unexpected challenge to the local authority care plan, which may also lead to increased expectations of contact arrangements. This can mean that the experience of the FfA carer may become more akin to that of a concurrent planning carer, whilst in other situations a concurrent carer may find that where birth parents make an early withdrawal from the assessment process, their experience is more akin to that envisaged for an FfA carer.

This has led to a number of agencies using the umbrella term of "early permanence carers" and "early permanence placements", and ensuring that all their carers receive a robust preparation and training programme that prepares them for all eventualities.

The Practice Guidance (Coram and BAAF, 2013) identified three principal issues:

1. Local authorities need to ensure that the identification of a child suitable for an FfA placement is based on evidence that has been properly gathered together, analysed, tested and agreed and clearly establishes the positive benefits to the child. Although the assessed likelihood of a child returning to their birth family should be minimal, it must be

recognised that, until the placement order is made, circumstances can change so the risk will always be there.

2. In making an FfA placement, the strengths of the carers and the support available to them must be clearly identified so that if a child returns to their birth family, the adults and child would recover from the distress caused. Loss and disruption are common experiences in family placement and impact on adults, but above all on children. FfA is intended to minimise the moves that children experience, but from time to time it may itself be caught up in them.
3. Although there are potential difficulties in implementing and using FfA as a route to permanence, accepting the current model of sequential placement planning for children cannot be justified.

KEY AREAS TO CONSIDER

From our discussions and through wider work being undertaken by Coram and the DfE, we would now identify the following key areas for a local authority to take account of when introducing FfA into their care planning process and developing their policy and procedures:

- **Ensure that there is senior management support** in children's services and the adoption and fostering services for developing early permanence and, where needed, a willingness to address any resistance or lack of understanding of this from outside agencies such as legal services, CAFCASS and the courts.
- **Arrange training events for all social work teams** across children's services, including IROs, so that all staff in the local authority understand the principles of early permanence and the benefits for children offered by making an FfA placement earlier in proceedings.
- **Establish "champions"** who can focus on the development work needed and who can be seen as "subject matter experts" to liaise with/mentor children's social workers involved in individual cases.
- **Set up early tracking systems for children**, overseen by senior managers with input from the adoption team, so that FfA can be considered for all children where adoption may be the plan, but also so that there is informed decision making about when the use of an FfA placement is appropriate for the individual child.
- **Provide clear written information and explanation for birth parents and their advocates** about the principles and processes of early permanence, including the identified benefits to the child, and reassurance that this will not disadvantage them in court proceedings.

- **Ensure that there is a specific focus on early permanence within the adoption recruitment strategy** and that workers involved in recruitment have a clear understanding of FfA as a potential route to adoption and of the differences and similarities to concurrent planning placements.
- **Develop recruitment materials that include information on FfA** to be used on all platforms – websites, social media and in all written information provided to prospective adopters from their earliest point of contact.
- **Include information about FfA in all training for prospective adopters**, but also provide additional training on FfA and early permanence for any prospective adopters considering FfA, alongside concurrent carers where the agency operates a concurrent planning scheme, so they have a clear understanding of the benefits, risks and uncertainties, what the fostering role entails, and how this may impact on them as individuals and as a family.
- **Recognise that FfA is not right for all adoptive families** and may not be right for all children.
- **Ensure that assessing social workers have a good knowledge of the issues raised for FfA carers** when carrying out the fostering role and address the additional areas for exploration – motivation to offer FfA, an understanding of what it means to "carry the risks of the placement" and manage the impact of uncertainty on themselves and their family.
- **Ensure that there is clear planning** when an FfA placement is being made so that full information is provided to FfA carers.
- **Provide social work support to the placement** which recognises the different impacts that are likely to occur for an FfA carer providing a fostering placement from that of a mainstream foster carer, as well as opportunities for peer support from other FfA carers.
- **Ensure that there is a robust matching process** when consent to adoption has been given through consent or a placement order, and that full information is provided to the FfA carers/prospective adopters, and adoption support needs identified for both the short and longer term.

FfA is still relatively new and whilst it is positive to see the contribution these placements are making to achieve added stability and reduced delay for children in achieving their permanent placement, it is important that agencies put in place mechanisms for reviewing and learning from every FfA case. It is also important that this learning is fed back to all parts of their service, as well as to the courts and judiciary so that they can revise or review their policies and procedures, where necessary. Whilst it is inevitable that a small number of children will return to the care of their birth family, and this should not necessarily be seen as a failure, these cases will have a significant impact on the FfA carers and it is important that lessons are learned for improved practice.

As practice continues to develop, policy-makers may need to look at whether existing policy, regulations and statutory guidance need to be amended to recognise the continuum that has developed for the use of early permanence placements. Another consideration is whether amendments are needed to include those currently not covered in existing guidance, for example, with sibling adopters through use of Reg. 24, or placements made following the making of a placement order where carers are currently unable to access the full range of support.

Coram and BAAF (2013) reflect that: **'Where FfA provides a fair, evidence based and just solution, it is a child-centred opportunity that is not to be missed'**.

It has been encouraging to see how this opportunity for children to achieve more timely security in their permanent placement through early permanence is being embraced as part of permanence planning for children and is becoming embedded into social work practice. We hope that this Good Practice Guide will be helpful in assisting those local authorities and adoption agencies that are still in the early stages of incorporating this into their practice, and will inform the further development that will come as RAAs begin to establish themselves.

FINAL THOUGHTS FROM CONCURRENT PLANNING AND FfA CARERS

CP1: Read everything you can first – and talk to others who have done it! And always, always be the strongest and most vocal advocate for your child that you can be. Use support and your networks.

CP2: We often give prospective adopters advice. We explain that it is the adults that are taking the risks and not the children. We say that it is a very hard place to be in because you care about the child, the birth parent and yourself and all those things are in conflict. We explain that it gives you an opportunity to meet and get the blessing of the birth parent. We have photos of ourselves with our son and his birth mother, which he can see. We tell them we think it is a brilliant process. We explain that he has been in the same home all his life and this helps him feel secure and means we have cared for him all that time. We say that as soon as you start caring for a baby you love it and they become like your own. It is therefore difficult to consider losing them – but that the best place for a baby will be with their birth parents if the court feels that is right. We explain that it is rare for an FfA child to go to its birth parent because often their lives are in a very difficult place, or their child would not be recommended for FfA. We reiterate that your job is to love the child whatever the outcome – that it is all about the child.

CP3: We absolutely recommend it for anyone who is sure that they can put the child's interests first and recognise that they can deal with the uncertainty better than the child can. It's high risk but very high reward. That also means that it's important to get as much information as you can about the child, from everyone you can.

CP4: If I take the time to reflect on our decision to become concurrent carers and then adopters, I'm certain it was the right decision for us, our family and for our adopted son. We totally adore him. And we feel it is a privilege to parent someone else's child and we are certain, at the moment, that it was the right decision for us.

FfA1: Really consider the emotional impact the process will have on you all. And recognise that there is a real risk that the child may not stay with you. But, that aside, go for it and hope that you'll be providing a permanent loving home for the child from as early as possible.

FfA2: It is the most natural way of adopting a child and so closely matches the experience of having a birth child; having done both, I can confidently say that this is the case. If you are prepared to take a risk and trust the authorities to make the right outcomes for children, then you have got nothing to lose, and at the very least, will have made a massive difference to a child for the first months of his life.

FfA3: We couldn't picture starting a family any other way. It was not without its challenges and stresses, but the rewards that we have got (all the firsts we have had, the joy of seeing our baby grow from being a day old and building such a strong attachment) could never be beaten. We are so grateful to have had this opportunity and feel blessed that it has happened.

FfA4: Do not think it is the easy option that means you can get a small baby! Please examine whether you want to do it for yourself or if you are really on board with thinking about what's best for the child and what might be best for both parents. Grill social workers about where the case is up to so you are clear and ask questions when you don't understand legal terms, etc. Do not think that it's just scaremongering to say that they may go back, because we know it can happen! For the sake of any other children, be cautious in how you describe the placement – make much of the value of fostering whether or not it heads to adoption, as then they [the children] are not having their view of you and your trustworthiness crushed if it falls through.

FfA5: It was the right decision for us and our family and we would definitely recommend anyone to do it; if we could guarantee such a positive outcome for us and our son, we'd do it again.

FfA6: Advise them that they need to prepare for a rollercoaster as there are constant changes throughout the process and the emotional stress is very difficult to deal with. They will need full support of family and friends to get through it, as we have had.

FfA7: Without a doubt the best thing we have done – it's challenging and couples need to be strong but the rewards are immense.

FfA8: Yes, we don't ever regret it – in fact we're currently going through the process again – though this time it's very different. It was definitely the right decision for our son.

FfA9: Just be totally aware of as many facts as possible, the risks and challenges such as contact visits. It has been the best thing for us as our child has been with us since he was only 20 hours old and he knows no different and the bond is strong. The positives overtake the negatives but they must have all the facts to make a decision.

FfA10: My advice would be to get as much information as possible and make sure social services tell you all the rules and regulations. Make sure that you know exactly what is required of you and always ask for worst case scenarios so you know where things stand. I would say it is not for the fainthearted or overly emotional, but if you can do it, it is so good for the child's long-term security and well-being.

FfA11: It's a great and wonderful way of adopting a child and giving her the best start in life.

FfA12: Go with your gut instinct. Don't rule it out. You have to have an understanding employer, willing to let you go at a moment's notice. You have to be able to afford to live without your income for as long as it takes. You have to stay strong and believe in what you are doing. But when you first hear about your child and see a picture, and you know they are meant to be your child, then you have no option but to go for it. Your child will come to you sooner than they would have done if you'd waited for [the child to be placed for] adoption and those extra precious months are invaluable.

Bibliography

Adams P (2012) *Planning for Contact in Permanent Placements*, London: BAAF

Argent H (2011) *Related by Adoption*, London: BAAF

Beek M and Schofield G (2004) *Providing a Secure Base in Long-Term Foster Care*, London: BAAF

Borthwick and Donnelly (2013) *Concurrent Planning: Achieving early permanence for babies and young children*, London: BAAF

Burnell A, Castell K and Cousins J (2009) *Siblings Together or Apart*, Practice Paper, London: Family Futures, available at: www.familyfutures.co.uk/wp-content/uploads/2012/11/Siblings-Together-or-Apart-Practice-Paper.pdf

CAFCASS (2013) *Good Practice Guidance for Adoption Agencies and CAFCASS: Children relinquished for adoption*, available at: www.cafcass.gov.uk/media/126321/good_practice_for_adoption_agencies_and_cafcass_-_children_relinquished_for_adoption.pdf

Coram and BAAF (2013) *Fostering for Adoption: Practice guidance*, available at: www.coram.org.uk/sites/default/files/resource_files/46%20Fostering%20for%20Adoption%20Guidance_2013.pdf

Coram (2013) *Outcomes of Concurrent Planning: Summary of findings*, available at: www.coram.org.uk/sites/default/files/resource_files/Concurrent%20Planning%20Report%20Summary%20%28Mar%202014%29%20FINAL.pdf

CoramBAAF (2015) *The Provision of Information to Fostering for Adoption Carers*, Practice Note 59, London: CoramBAAF

Department for Education (2010) *Care Planning, Placement and Case Review Regulations*, London: DfE

Department for Education (2011) *Fostering Services (England) Regulations 2011*, London: DfE

Department for Education (2013) *Statutory Guidance on Adoption for Local Authorities, Voluntary Adoption Agencies and Adoption Support Agencies*, London: DfE

Department for Education (2013a) *Adoption Agencies (Miscellaneous Amendments) Regulations*, London: DfE

Department for Education (2013b) *Care Planning, Placement and Case Review and Fostering Services (Miscellaneous Amendments) Regulations 2013*, London: DfE

Department for Education (2014) *Statutory Guidance on Adoption for Local Authorities, Voluntary Adoption Agencies and Adoption Support Agencies (draft)*, London: DfE

Department for Education (2014a) *Statutory Guidance on Adoption for Local Authorities, Voluntary Adoption Agencies and Adoption Support Agencies, Early Permanence Placements and Approval of Prospective Adopters as Foster Carers*, London: DfE

Department for Education (2014b) *Adoption and Care Planning (Miscellaneous Amendments) Regulations*, London: DfE

Department for Education (2014c) *Early Permanence Placements and Approval of Prospective Adopters as Foster Carers: Statutory guidance for local authorities and adoption agencies*, London: DfE

Department for Education (2015) *Care Planning and Fostering (Miscellaneous Amendments) (England) Regulations*, London: DfE

Department for Education (2015a) *Children Act 1989 Guidance and Regulations Volume 2: Care planning, placement and case review*, London: DfE

Dibben E (2017) *Undertaking an Adoption Assessment: A guide to collecting and analysing information for the Prospective Adopter's Report (PAR) England* (3rd edn), London: BAAF

Dibben E and Howorth V (2016) *Adoption by Foster Carers: A guide to preparing, assessing and supporting foster carers adopting children in their care*, London: CoramBAAF

Family Rights Group (2014a) *What is a Family Group Conference?*, Advice Sheet 3, available at: www.frg.org.uk/images/Advice_Sheets/3-what-is-a-family-group-conference.pdf

Family Rights Group (2014b) *Adoption: What does it mean for birth parents?*, Advice Sheet 23, available at: www.frg.org.uk/images/Advice_Sheets/23-adoption-of-children-looked-after-by-the-local-authority.pdf

Greenwood M and McGregor J (2011) *Improving the Life Chances of Children: A model for intervention led pre-birth assessments*, Leeds: Leeds City Council, available at: http://leedschildcare.proceduresonline.com/pdfs/epp_resource_pack.pdf

Humphreys C and Kiraly M (2011) 'High-frequency family contact: a road to nowhere for infants', *Child & Family Social Work*, 16:1, pp 1–11

Kenrick J (2010) 'Concurrent planning: a retrospective study of the continuities and discontinuities of care, and their impact on the development of infants and young children placed for adoption by the Coram Concurrent Planning Project', *Adoption & Fostering*, 33:4, pp 5–18

Leeds City Council (2015) *Early Permanence Placements: Project resource pack*, Leeds: Leeds City Council

Lord J and Cullen D (2016) *Effective Adoption Panels* (7th edn), London: BAAF

Millar I and Paulson-Ellis C (2009) *Exploring Infertility Issues in Adoption*, London: BAAF

National Adoption Leadership Board (2014) *Impact of Court Judgements on Adoption: What the judgements do and do not say*, available at: www.first4adoption.org.uk/wp-content/uploads/2014/11/ALB-Impact-of-Court-Judgments-on-Adoption-November-2014.pdf

National Adoption Service for Wales and AFA Cymru (2016) *Fostering to Adopt Practice Guidance*, available at: www.afacymru.org/index.php/en/professionals/policy-and-guidance/adoption

Schofield G and Beek M (2014a) *Promoting Attachment and Resilience: A guide for foster carers and adopters on using the Secure Base Model*, London: BAAF

Schofield G and Beek M (2014b) *The Secure Base Model: Promoting attachment and resilience in foster care and adoption*, London: BAAF

Further resources

www.youtube.com/watch?v=3e120dRjhNI – Coram concurrent planning film with carers talking

www.youtube.com/watch?v=vrLAwXbMArA – Adoptive mother Angela discusses concurrent planning with Coram (radio interview)

www.youtube.com/watch?v=VqPl9j7jSr0 – Preparing for Concurrent Planning film of carers talking (Adoption Matters)

www.youtube.com/watch?v=34DxtoeQpY0 – Dealing with the uncertainty of concurrent planning (film of carers talking) (Adoption Matters)

www.adoptionmatters.org/blog/surviving-thriving-when-baby-is-returned-home/?utm_content=buffer8f53c&utm_medium=social&utm_source=twitter.com&utm_campaign=buffer – blog from a single concurrent carer where the baby was returned to her birth father.

Appendix 1
Early permanence carers

The following carers (coded CP for concurrent planning, and FfA for Fostering for Adoption) are quoted within the text.

CP1 lives with her husband and adopted daughter, now aged eight, who was placed with them when she was two days old via concurrent planning. Their daughter has never lived with anyone else but did have contact experiences that were described as being deeply traumatic and have left her with anxiety and low self-esteem. She is currently receiving extensive therapy from CAMHS funded by the ASF.

CP2 lives with her husband and two adopted children aged 9 and 12; the children are unrelated by birth. Their eldest child was placed via concurrent planning aged eight weeks; he had lived at the hospital before being placed as he was withdrawing from drugs. The fostering placement lasted for one year and three months before their child was matched with them at adoption panel.

CP3 are a couple who live with their adopted son, now aged three. Their son was placed with them via concurrent planning aged one week, after being discharged from hospital. After four months of placement, he was matched with them for adoption.

CP4 lives with her husband, birth daughter aged eight and adopted son aged four. Their son spent his first few days in hospital with his birth mother, and then 36 hours with her in a mother and baby unit, and remained in the unit being looked after by a foster carer until he was placed with CP4 at 10 weeks old via concurrent planning. After six months in placement, he was matched with them for adoption, and six months later the adoption order was granted.

FfA1 lives with her husband and four adopted children. The couple adopted three children in 2012, now aged 12, 11 and 9. The local authority contacted the family six weeks before the birth of their children's sibling to ask them to consider an FfA placement. The child was placed with the family when she was 36 hours old, and was matched with them for adoption after she had been in placement for one year.

FfA2 lives with her husband, one birth child and two adopted children. The family had adopted one child initially and was asked to consider her sibling as an FfA placement. There was some delay in placing the child as the local authority only found out about the pregnancy in the very late stages and DBS checks needed to be renewed; therefore the child was placed with alternative foster carers for the first five weeks of his life. The child was matched with them for adoption after being in placement for four months, and he is now aged two-and-a-half.

FfA3 are a couple who live with their adopted son, now aged 11 months. The couple met their baby at the hospital when he was one day old, after an interim care order was granted; they spent the next three days at hospital with him before being able to bring him home. After four months in placement, he was matched with them for adoption.

FfA4 lives with her husband and three adopted children. The couple adopted twin girls, now aged six, through the normal adoption process when they were 11 months old. The couple then had an FfA placement, who was three days old when placed but after eight weeks returned to the care of his birth parents. A second FfA placement was identified when he was five months old, but delays due to an additional residential assessment meant that he was not placed until he was eight months old. He was in placement for 10 weeks before being matched with them for adoption and is now aged 16 months.

FfA5 are a couple who live with their adopted son. Their son was placed with them aged five months, and for the 10 days prior to this had been placed with emergency foster carers when he was taken into care. After four months in placement, he was matched with them for adoption, and 18 months after that the adoption order was granted.

FfA6 lives with her husband and their adopted child, who is aged 12 months. The child was in the neonatal unit for three weeks before being placed with the couple, and was in placement for nine months before being matched with them for adoption.

FfA7 and his wife live with their adopted daughter, who is now aged 18 months. Their child was a relinquished baby whom they met when she was two hours old and who was placed with them immediately. The couple had been pre-matched with two siblings but this placement fell through so even though they had originally ruled out FfA, they thought the chance of success outweighed the risk. After four months of being in placement, she was matched with them for adoption.

FfA8 are a couple who live with their adopted son, who is now aged three. Their son was placed with them after spending his first three weeks in hospital, and was in placement for eight months before being matched with them for adoption.

FfA9 are a couple who live with their adopted son, who is now aged two. Their son was removed at birth from his birth mother as she was in prison at the time for child neglect. He was placed with them on the day he was born and after five months in placement was matched with them for adoption. The couple also have a step-son from a previous relationship who spends time at the home.

FfA10 are a couple who live with their three birth children, aged 12, 10 and 7, and two adopted children, aged three and two. Their youngest child was placed with them aged two months, after being placed with other foster carers for three weeks when he was discharged from hospital. After seven months in placement, he was matched with them for adoption.

FfA11 lives with her three birth children and one adopted daughter, now aged one. Her daughter was placed with her when she was eight hours old, after being removed from her birth mother.

FfA12 are a couple who live with their birth daughter, aged six, and their adopted son, aged two. Their son moved in with them in 2015, when he was 15 weeks old. He was matched with them after about three months. He had been placed from birth with his birth mother in a parent and child foster placement. When it became clear that his birth mother couldn't keep him safe, after a few weeks she left the placement and he was then moved to them under an FfA arrangement.

Appendix 2
Early permanence screening matrix

Yes	No	If yes, name of parent/s	Criteria to be assessed in conjunction with Core Assessment
☐	☐		Parent has killed or seriously harmed another child through abuse or neglect and no significant change has occurred since
☐	☐		Child has experienced extreme physical or sexual abuse by the parent/s (or parent/s have allowed someone else to abuse the child) and must be removed from the home
☐	☐		Parental rights to another child have been involuntarily terminated (e.g. adoption order or court order) following a period of service delivery to the parents and no significant change has occurred since
☐	☐		Child or siblings/s have been in care on at least one other occasion for a period of three months or more with child protection involvement
☐	☐		Parent/s have been diagnosed with severe mental illness and have not responded to previously delivered mental health services. Symptoms continue that prevent parent/s from being able to physically and emotionally meet the needs of the child
☐	☐		There have been two separate incidents of child protection involvement or there is a chronic/ historical pattern of abuse or severe neglect

☐	☐		Parent/s have a history of substance abuse or are chemically dependent on non-prescription substances and/or have a history of treatment failures
☐	☐		Child had been abandoned with friend, relatives, foster care or hospital or, after being placed in care, parent/s disappear or visit/attend contact rarely, erratically or not at all
☐	☐		Parent/s have shown significant deficits in caring for child, or previous children, and have poor or non-existent support system of relatives/friends to share parenting
☐	☐		There is a pattern of documented domestic violence between the parents (or partners) and they refuse to separate
☐	☐		Parent is under the age of 16 with no parenting support systems, and placement of the child and parent together has failed (or is likely to fail) due to the parent's behaviour
☐	☐		Parent has asked to relinquish the child on more than one occasion following initial intervention
☐	☐		Family members have been considered/assessed and ruled out as potential carers for the child
☐	☐		Other parent has been assessed and ruled out as a potential carer for the child
☐	☐		Adopters of sibling/s have been approached and do not wish to be considered to adopt the child

This is an appropriate case to be considered for an early permanence care plan.

	Name	**Date**
Child's social worker		
Children and families team manager		
Adoption team manager		

Reproduced with kind permission of Gloucestershire County Council (originally adapted from a CCS Adoption document)

Appendix 3
Early permanence planning: referral form

PART ONE – to be completed by child's social worker when requesting an early permanence placement

Name of social worker making referral, Team name/location and contact details	
Name of team manager Has this referral been discussed with the team manager?	
Name of allocated permanence social worker (if applicable)	

Name/s of child or children being referred	
DOB (or estimated DOB)	
Geographical location of immediate birth family	
Geographical location of extended birth family	
Geographical location of significant other	
Names of prospective carers	[To be completed by adoption team]
Location of prospective carers	[To be completed by adoption team]

Reason for accommodation	
Why is an early permanence care plan appropriate in this case?	
Legal position (including proposed plans) Please provide dates of any court hearings or legal planning meetings known at current time	
What is the Guardian's view of this proposed early permanence placement?	

PART TWO – Child's needs, to be completed by child's social worker, and proposed carer's ability to meet these needs, to be completed in conjunction with adoption team social worker

	Child's needs:	**Carer's ability to meet needs:**
Are there any known or expected disabilities? If yes, please provide details		
Are there any additional health needs? If yes, please provide details		
Provide details of any medical or genetic issues known about birth parents		
Are there any specific needs for this child in relation to ethnicity, culture, language or religion? If so, please specify		
Brief physical description of parents		
Brief physical description of child or children		
Pre birth/pre placement experiences (including description of birth family lifestyle)		
Safeguarding needs – are there any identified risk factors? If yes, outline risks and contingency plans		
Does this child/children have any other siblings? Have any siblings on maternal or paternal side been adopted? If so, provide details		
Are there any specific birth family wishes regarding the early permanence family?		

Do the birth parents wish to meet the FfA carers prior to placement? If yes, has this been risk assessed?		
Any views of significant others that should be known?		
Are there any identified connected persons who could potentially care for the child? If yes, please provide full details		
Have all viability assessments been completed? If no, what is the timescale for these and who is still being considered?		
Are there any special skills required of the FfA carers?		
What are the contact arrangements for birth parents or any siblings? If not known, what is being proposed? Where will contact take place? Will arrangements be made for contact handovers to be completed by contact centre workers?		

PART THREE – To be completed at linking meeting to consider whether this placement should become an adoption placement

Meeting attendees: **Date:**		
	Child's needs:	**Carer's ability to meet needs:**
Are there any specific financial needs in relation to the child/children or prospective adopters?		

What are their support networks?		
Has carer demonstrated an ability to work with the local authority?		
What are the carer's attitudes to the particular circumstances or ability of the child/children in the FfA placement?		
What are the carer's views on sharing the child/ children's life story?		
Are there any post-adoption support needs identified?		
Please note any other relevant information		

Summary of information
Are all parties agreed that this is a suitable match? Briefly describe the main factors contributing to this decision
Proposed plan and timescales

Reproduced with kind permission of Gloucestershire County Council

Appendix 4
Concurrency and Fostering for Adoption checklist for social workers

A "Suitable for FfA" decision needs to be based on evidence that has been properly gathered and analysed, the decision appropriately reasoned and recorded having attention to *Re B-S* considerations.

In considering all aspects of concurrency and FfA, **the child's needs and welfare are paramount**.

Name of child:

Date of birth:

Carefirst ID:

Decision-making meeting:

Date:

Attendance:

Chair (this should be CC team manager or CC service manager)

Child care social worker:

Adoption/permanence team manager:

Family finder:

IRO:

CHILD	Yes	No	N/A	Comment	Any relevant date
Is the local authority "considering adoption" for this child?					
Have previous children of birth parent/s been removed? What is their status? Adopted?					
Has there been a permanency planning meeting? (This is from three months gestation)					
Has there been a pre-birth assessment?					
What other assessments are ongoing/planned for?					
Has CAFCASS Plus* involvement been considered from 20 weeks pregnancy?					
Has there been a Family Group Conference/ meeting exploring others in the network? Family and friends ruled out? Initial viability assessments (IVAs) outstanding?					
Has there been a legal planning meeting to discuss the case?					
Has there been consideration of paternity issues? Has paternity been confirmed? What plans are there to establish paternity?					
Are the care plan and social work evidence template (SWET) ready pre-birth?					
Is the child relinquished?					
Is the child subject to an interim care order, any other order or subject to proceedings?					
If the child is Section 20, the parents need to agree to an FfA placement. Have the parents agreed? Note re: case of *Re CA – 2012 EWHC 2190 (Fam) – High Court – Hedley J:* social worker must be satisfied of the capacity of the person giving s.20 consent and that they are fully informed.					

* CAFCASS Plus is a pilot scheme in Lincolnshire in which CAFCASS is involved with some families at an earlier stage than normal, where a local authority is considering making an application for care proceedings.

CHILD	Yes	No	N/A	Comment	Any relevant date
Parents (including birth father without PR) or any other person whose wishes and feelings the local authority consider to be relevant (s.22(4)) to be notified of the implications of their child being placed in an FfA/concurrency placement. A specific letter about the local authority considering FfA should be sent and reasons (including avoiding placement moves) given. Parents advised to gain legal representation. In addition to including this in all initial and subsequent care plans, we currently recommend that the following is stated: should the local authority progress to a single plan of adoption, then consideration will be given to an FfA/concurrency placement. Counselling to be offered to the parents where such placement is being considered. Refer to birth parent counsellor? Record the date and resource offered and parent's response.					
If parents do not agree, then an interim care order is needed before the local authority can progress to an FfA or concurrency placement.					
Has there been discussion with the IRO? The LAC review can be bought forward View of the IRO View of the Guardian, if appointed					
Single plan of adoption? (Not needed for concurrency.)					
Refer to Nominated Officer who needs to approve the FfA decision. Nominated Officer to be made aware of parent's views.					
Early consideration of how the child will be told Any direct work/support necessary? The child's wishes and feelings need to be recorded.					

FfA/CONCURRENCY CARERS	Yes	No	N/A	Comment	Any relevant date
Reg. 25A of the Care Planning, Placement and Case Review (England) Regulations 2010 enables approved prospective adopters by both local authorities and VAAs to be temporarily approved as foster carers for a named child by the local authority with responsibility for that child without having to be approved as foster carers. This will not apply if the adopters have already been approved as foster carers via dual approval panel for concurrency. Necessary paperwork is to be completed by the child care social worker and adoption social worker following selection of suitable prospective adopters and before the placement can proceed.					
Consideration of other children in the identified carer's family and the impact of placement (e.g. where siblings to be placed with other birth sibling now adopted).					
Carers need to be fully informed about the nature of the placement, their role as foster carers and that the court can decide an alternative plan to adoption. Specific relevant training provided by adoption service. Adopters to then sign a declaration at this point that explicitly states their understanding of their responsibilities as foster carers and of the risks associated with FfA.					
Evidence of the carer having understanding of both the fostering and adoption role? Joint visit by fostering and adoption team workers. This will be done at the point of the plan being progressed.					
Preparation of carer/s (having regard to any urgency of the placement)? Are the social workers confident that the carers fully understand the task of taking a child under FfA?					
All necessary training has been completed. This will be done at the point of the plan being progressed					

PLANNING FOR AFTER PLACEMENT	Yes	No	N/A	Comment	Any relevant date
Appropriate support and visits by child's social worker and the adoption and/or fostering supervising social worker. This will be done at the point of the plan being progressed.					
LAC review for single plan of adoption					
Placement is under fostering regulations: Need to continue process of: - adoption medical - BID (best interest decision) - ADM - placement order					
After placement order obtained, attend matching panel to consider "suitability of the match" (s.33 Adoption Agency Regulations 2005).					

Differences and similarities between concurrency and FfA

CONCURRENCY	FfA
Birth family	**Birth family**
Possible rehabilitation plan	No rehabiltiation plan
No outstanding initial viability assessments	No outstanding initial viability assessments
Could be an ongoing parenting assessment but likely to be negative	No ongoing parenting assessments – all concluded
Paternity to be established, but if not known can consider continuing with a warning that this may be an issue.	Paternity to be established, but if not known can consider continuing with a warning that this may be an issue
No single plan of adoption yet	Single plan of adoption by local authority
Adopters	**Adopters**
Dual approval through permanence panel	Advice only from panel
No need for temporary approval by Nominated Officer	Need for temporary approval by Nominated Officer
Full name and address of carers must not be given out	Anonymity of adopters to be protected as there is a single plan of adoption – no use of surname or address given out
Carers should support contact arrangements	Carers should support contact arrangements

Face-to-face meeting with birth parents to be promoted whenever possible. A lot of comfort can be given to the birth parent to know who the child is placed with. Safety and security of carers and placement to be considered.	Face-to-face meeting with birth parents to be promoted wherever possible. A lot of comfort can be given to the birth parent to know who the child is placed with. Safety and security of carers and placement to be considered.
Carer will be actively promoting the potential rehabilitation plan as well as able to go forward with adoption if this becomes the plan for the child	No active rehabilitation plan

Decision with analysis:

Signature of Chair:

Reproduced with kind permission of Northamptonshire County Council

Appendix 5
Early permanence placements: information for health care professionals

This content is taken from a leaflet provided to health care professionals by Leeds City Council.

Early permanence placements explained

If it is identified that the child will be at risk in being cared for by their birth parents or other family members, then the local authority will make the decision to place the child with foster carers at the earliest opportunity, which can be from birth or soon after. Early permanence placements are where the child is placed with approved adopters who are also approved as foster carers. The aim of such placements is to prevent moves for the child during the temporary period of foster care and between foster carers and adopters, should the courts agree the plan for adoption.

The carers may be dually approved as foster carers and adopters from the outset, or might be approved prospective adopters who have been temporarily approved as foster carers for a named child under Reg. 25A of the Care Planning, Placement and Case Review (England) Regulations 2010 ("2010 Regulations"). The foster carers are aware that their role is part of a process. They and all professionals will need to remain child-focused, remembering that they are working towards the best outcome for the child, whether this is rehabilitation with the birth family or adoption.

If the court decides that the child should be returned to live with their birth parents or should be placed with family members, the carers will support the child's move. If the court decides that the plan is for adoption, then the child will remain permanently with these foster carers who will go on to adopt the child. This minimises the negative impact of separation for the adopted child.

Health professional involvement in pre-birth planning

Early identification of possible appropriate placements is crucial to the service in providing the best opportunities for the child and most local authorities have practice guidance on undertaking pre-birth assessments. A multi-disciplinary pre-birth intervention and assessment should start as early as possible to avoid delays. It is important that birth parents feel that they are part of a fair process and that they are supported and enabled to be part of the child's plan to achieve this.

The midwifery service is likely to be a key source of such referrals. It should be noted that many women with whom local authorities become involved may not have accessed antenatal services at all.

Health professionals, including obstetricians, GPs, health visitors, safeguarding practitioners and Family Nurse Practitioners (FNPs) will be involved in recognising risks and concerns about the parent's circumstances and ability to protect the child from harm during and after pregnancy. They should refer to Children's Services as soon as they know of a pregnancy where there may be a risk of parents being unable to care for their child.

In early permanence placements, it is likely that the full health information about the child has not been collated or yet known. All health professionals need to gather and share information that would be relevant to the well-being and health of the child in the future. Information such as family history of genetic illness, antenatal substance and alcohol misuse or blood-borne viral infection are risk factors that should be shared with the medical adviser for the adoption agency. The role of the medical adviser is crucial in being able to share what health information is available. A key aspect is to help foster carers and birth parents understand the uncertainties of the future prognosis and present a balanced picture of the known risks.

This situation is different to other permanent placements where there will have been an opportunity for all medical information to be evaluated and assessed, with further investigations if needed, and shared with prospective carers. This is likely to have been concluded before a placement is made.

Health professional involvement in the perinatal period

Interdisciplinary and interagency working and input is crucial in early permanency in helping to identify any issues related to the parents before and at the time of the child's birth. Health professionals who may be involved include GPs, midwives, obstetricians, neonatology doctors, FNPs and other staff who may be involved in providing specialist services. These issues would be shared when invited to attend a care team/core group meeting, a pre-birth assessment meeting or a LAC review. At these times, it is important that the health professional is aware of these issues in relation to the implications of early permanency for the birth parents, carers and child.

The foster carers and birth parents will have their own support systems through Children's Services but the additional, unbiased support from health professionals will be paramount to them.

Health professional involvement post-placement

When a placement is made with the foster carers, it is possible that they will not have fostered or parented before, and while they will have received specialist training and a rigorous assessment, it can be an anxious time for them. It is also an uncertain time for them and the birth parents while the courts make the decision about the child's future. The ethos behind early permanence placements is that the adults involved, i.e. the carers and birth parents, take on the strain and stress of this uncertainty, and not the child. The foster carers will be very aware that their role is part of a process that is working towards the best outcome for the child, which will cause additional pressure or worry for them. They are trying to make a bond with a child whom they hope to care for in the future whilst still being expected to take and collect the child from any contact to maintain attachment to the birth parents, should the child return to them.

The early permanence carers will be carefully prepared and supported to undertake this emotionally challenging role. However, it is important that all professionals involved in the case are aware that while they are foster carers and are expected to fulfil all the obligations of foster carers, their need for support, confidentiality and training will differ from other foster carers as there are aspects to their role that are very different. Thus, for example, these carers are being asked to make a long-term emotional commitment to the child while at the same time not only managing the uncertainty of the outcome, but also actively supporting the planning for the possible rehabilitation to the birth family.

In order for the carers to build strong attachments to the child, they will need support from health and Children's Services. The carers will be expected to meet the child's health and social needs whilst providing a nurturing and secure placement under the frequent oversight of professionals. This oversight relates to the child in care, who will potentially have a higher level of uncertainty of health needs due to the past medical history. Therefore, in addition to routine health visitor and medical checks plus immunisations, there will be additional statutory assessments provided by health professionals providing looked after children's initial and review health assessments.

When the process works well, one carer was able to comment about her health visitor: 'She was my rock; she was so reassuring and gave me confidence in my parenting as well as understanding how I was feeling' (quoted in *Concurrent Planning*, Borthwick and Donnelly, 2013).

Health professionals, including midwives, health visitors, GPs and hospital staff will be encouraged to refer to Children's Services as soon as they know that a woman might be at risk of not being able to care for her child.

Children's Services will be expected to allocate the referral as soon as it is possible with no built-in delays. If you have any concerns that are not being addressed expediently, please inform the appropriate senior manager.

Confidentiality is a real concern for carers in early permanence placements as these carers are possibly going to go on to adopt the child in their care. It is essential that the carers' full details, including surname and address, are kept confidential at all times. Birth family members must not be given any details other than the carers' first names. Extra care should be taken when sending any written correspondence, and reports to the birth family are not to include the carers' confidential details.

Reproduced with kind permission of Leeds City Council

Appendix 6
Consideration for contact arrangements for children in Fostering for Adoption placements

All cases should be assessed on an individual basis, considering the child and circumstances in which they came into care. The baby or toddler may need time to settle into the placement before contact with their birth parents begins. Where appropriate and achievable, a meeting between the birth parent/s and the carers should occur prior to contact commencing.

There are some key practical considerations that will need to be managed, including:

- The **frequency of contact** – in some cases up to five times a week; three times a week appears more usual with contacts lasting between two–three hours. Coram's review of the concurrent planning programme found that the duration of contact arrangements averaged between 12 and 23 weeks.
- **Suitable contact centres and skilled contact supervisors** are needed in order to manage contact safely and sensitively. The carer will bring the child to contact, and the supervisors need to support the handovers between carers and parents, and manage any anxiety or tensions that arise. It is **important to have continuity of contact supervisor** for the child's sake, but also for the reassurance of the parents and carers.
- Supervisors will need to have some experience of managing the dynamics of contact arrangements and, whilst showing empathy to the birth parents, should be able to maintain a professional view as to how contact is progressing.
- There should be **at least two identified contact supervisors** so that if one is on leave or sick an identifiable contact supervisor is available.
- A **Strengths and Risk Assessment** is to be completed before contact arrangements are finalised, to ensure that supervisors are aware, and so that any perceived risks are identified and protective steps taken.

- **Who will be attending contact?** Will the birth family attend together or, if separated, will separate contacts need to be arranged? This may then impact on the child's routine.
- **Arrangements need to be made in respect of who arrives first and who leaves first** (including carers and the child). What are the arrangements for the handover – will the birth parents be in the contact centre 10 minutes before the child arrives, to ensure that no handover takes place in a public area? Will the birth parents leave first, with a check that they have left before the carers and child leave?
- Issues around the **location of the contact centre** in relation to the distance from the placement need to be considered. Are there any other transport issues, e.g. is there a need for a safety seat/car seat? Is there a contact centre or venue nearer to the birth parents' home than to the carers' home, to support the confidentiality of the placement? This should be considered alongside the length of time that the child may be in a car and the risk factors in maintaining confidentiality.
- A **contact schedule** must be put into place and reviewed regularly to ensure that it is meeting the child's needs.
- **Will the parents be able to feed and change the child during contact?** The carers should supply the equipment; no food or milk should be brought by the parents.
- If the carers are going to enter the contact centre, consideration should be given to their **signing in and not using their last name**.
- There could be a **contact book** so that the carers and parents can record what they did during contact: if a feed took place, if photos were taken, and if gifts were given.
- The **contact supervisor/s will take the contact notes**/recording of contact. How will these be shared? It is important that the matters recorded are consistent from one contact session to another, irrespective of the supervisor. This can be crucial evidence for the court and so an agreed format should be used.
- **How to manage goodbyes** – it can be difficult for birth parents to see the carers giving hugs and kisses to their child.
- **Consideration of use of mobile phones:** whether these are to be used by birth parents, relatives or carers in contact should be considered from the beginning. Discussion is needed about arrangements to provide photos and prevent photos being taken of the carers.
- **Think about gifts from birth parents:** does this need to be limited to small manageable items? If the birth parents buy clothes for the child, do they want them returned if the child has outgrown them?

- **If the parents are not consistent in attending contact**, will arrangements be made for cancelling with the carers and contact supervisors, so that the child is not brought to contact unnecessarily?
- Carers should be given advice on how to claim **travel expenses** (likely to be addressed in training).
- Carers and birth parents should be made aware of **social media** and the implications this may have in the case.

Reproduced with kind permission of Essex Social Care Academy

Appendix 7
Early permanence: information for parents

Most parents reading this leaflet will know that the local authority plans for your baby to be looked after by foster carers. The court will be making decisions about your child's future and you may be feeling angry, sad or confused. You are probably worried about what is going to happen to your child in care. This leaflet provides information about involving you as a parent in planning for your child's future.

Early permanence placements

An early permanence placement is a new way of working with families. It is a programme to help parents and children in situations where there are care proceedings and long-term plans for the children to be made. The aim is to reduce the number of moves and changes children experience while living away from their parent/s to make sure that your child has the best possible care while his or her long-term future is decided.

Staying in a temporary foster home is not always good for young children, especially if they have to move several more times while waiting for the decisions to be made. This is bound to make it more difficult for a child to settle when the court makes a decision, whether they return to their parent's care, go to relatives or are later placed for adoption. The use of early permanent placements in Essex offers children a different experience. Our main concern is the well-being of your child and if possible we would like to return him or her to live with you or to be cared for by another relative.

These families are committed to helping us to reunite parents with their children if this is possible. However, if the court decides that your child cannot return home to you or another member of your family, these dually approved carers are ready to offer the child the security of adoption without facing another move.

What we will offer you as parents

We will complete a pre-birth assessment, but we will not carry out a further parenting assessment unless this is ordered by the court. The court will decide what other assessments you need to have, if any, and when reports must be completed so there are no unnecessary delays.

We will provide a written agreement setting out contact arrangements, what you are expected to do and what help is available. We will provide opportunities for contact with your child in one of our contact centres with one of our contact supervisors. The decision about how often you see your child is made by our social work team who will consult with you and the Independent Reviewing Officer and ultimately the contact plan will be agreed at court. We will provide opportunities to develop parenting skills (if our assessment recommends this). We will provide help with practical arrangements.

What could happen to your child?

The court will decide whether your child can return to you or another member of your family. The decision will be based on the evidence from social workers, the Children's Guardian, and any other professional who has been asked to do an assessment or give an opinion. You will also be able to tell the court why you think your child should return to your care.

If the court decides that your child cannot return to you or a member of your extended family, then the best plan will be for your child to have the security of adoption by people who are already familiar to you and your child. This would avoid an upsetting move for your child.

You would already know the carers and we hope you would feel confident that they would give your child the love and security he or she needs. We hope that you would also feel that the carers respect and understand you and will be able to tell your child later that you love him or her, but that you had problems that made it hard for you to look after them.

Carers will be specially selected and trained

It will be their job to help support you by keeping the relationship going with your child. You will be able to meet them and get to know them when they bring your child to contact. They will be able to tell you what is happening to your child and what progress he or she is making.

The professionals

A social worker will be happy to explain this information in more detail. You may find it helpful to discuss the leaflet with your solicitor.

Reproduced with kind permission of Essex County Council

Appendix 8
Fostering for Adoption workbook

The following text has been adapted from a workbook published by Families for Children.

Introduction

Fostering for Adoption (FfA) was introduced to enable the placement of babies and young children whilst they were still in care proceedings (i.e. whilst the court is deciding whether they could return to the care of their birth parents or extended family members or would need to be placed for adoption), with families who could become their permanent families. FfA is used for children where the local authority has taken the decision that adoption is the right plan, based on all known information to prevent unnecessary moves for children in foster care and to promote early attachments. However, the possibility would always remain that during the court proceedings, there would be a different view taken or additional information might become available leading, in a very few cases, to the child returning to the care of his or her birth family. Relinquished babies whose mother/parents have not yet given their formal consent to adoption are also being placed for FfA till that consent has been given.

This workbook is designed to help you think through whether you feel that FfA would be a route you could consider in becoming an adopter. It will cover some of the areas you may have already discussed with your assessing social worker in a more generic sense, but in working through the questions and scenarios in this booklet, you will have the opportunity to think in more depth about the issues arising from FfA placements and whether this is right for you.

The questions are designed to be considered by yourselves, and then discussed with your social worker. This information would be incorporated into your PAR.

There are no right or wrong answers – but we hope that in taking the time to think carefully about the areas outlined, you will be able to come to a considered decision about whether taking a child under these regulations is right for you. You would always have the right to consider any child referred once you are approved on a case-by-case basis.

1. Motivation

We felt very much as if we were the ones who had to carry the risk for the baby... he had everything to gain by being with us from an early age. (FfA adopters)

Whether he stayed with us or not... this was our chance to do something amazing for him. To give him the best start. (FfA adopters)

(a) Why do you feel that FfA could be something you would like to consider? What do you feel you would gain from having a child placed under this process? What would the child gain?

2. Uncertainty

FfA placements are usually undertaken due to a reasonable amount of evidence, both current and historical, suggesting fundamental difficulties in the birth family making it unlikely that they will be able to successfully parent that child over time. Therefore, these are probably some of the most challenging families, coming with a wide variety of problems and possibly long-standing patterns of poor parenting across the generations. Parents may also have a history of mental illness or chronic drug and alcohol misuse. This means that babies born to these families are very vulnerable and at risk from day one, and may have undiagnosed extra needs. They need the most stable and secure placements as early as can be arranged.

When taking such a young baby, there is no certainty at all of how he or she will develop over time. We will have no clear indication of the impact of early stage neglect, and what the resultant behaviours and difficulties might be. It is important to remember that the placement is not guaranteed as the court hearing has not concluded yet – and there is still a possibility that the baby could be returned to his or her birth family.

a) How do you think you will manage living with that uncertainty, and not just in the short term?

b) What do you think your coping mechanisms might entail?

c) If a baby is placed with you under FfA regulations, your role is that of a foster carer. You would not share parental responsibility with the local authority. You would not be a party to the court proceedings. You would be caring for the baby, but would have no say in important decisions. You would have regular social work visits and would need to comply with additional directives from the court, for example, if contact with a member of the birth family was then needed. How do you think being told how to care for the baby would make you feel?

d) How do you think you would manage having to undertake tasks such as taking the child for direct contact with his or her birth family? Who would support you?

e) Contact could be expected to happen three times a week or more. How would you manage this emotionally and practically?

f) What if you didn't agree with what was being asked of you, for example, if the birth parent wanted the baby to wear particular clothes or eat a branded baby food? How might you deal with this?

g) If the baby is having contact with his or her birth parents or relatives, you would not be present during the contact. How would you cope with any emotions this could cause and who could you turn to for support?

h) How would you manage if the baby were returned to his or her birth family? What strategies might you use?

i) How would you support the baby during this time and what support would you then need from your family, friends and professionals?

j) If you have birth children already in your family, or other adopted children who may even be the siblings of the baby being placed under FfA, how would you support them to understand this process?

k) As future plans for the child remain uncertain, confidentiality for him or her is even more important, and you would not be able to share details of the child's background, or the reasons why he or she is unable to be with his or her birth family. This would include not being able to share details with those you would generally turn to for support. How would you manage this?

3. Grief and loss

In your preparation training you will have been asked to reflect on your own personal previous experiences of grief and loss. Even a very young baby will experience loss of his or her birth mother, which may impact over time on their sense of self.

a) How might your own experiences of loss be triggered by the loss of a baby, if he or she was returned to his or her birth family?

b) Do you think the fear of loss might make you less inclined to fully engage with the child during the time you are fostering them?

4. Flexibility – emotional and practical

These placements can happen very quickly. You may find out about a baby on a Monday and they could move in by the following weekend. On a practical level, this could mean giving very short notice at work, having to rush about buying essentials, changing holiday plans, and readjusting your life in a very short time frame. On an emotional level, this may result in a shift in the balance of a relationship, in your sense of professional identity, feeling scrutinised, and having expectations put on you.

a) How flexible do you think you will be able to be regarding purely practical issues?

b) What issues do you think might arise from the emotional flexibility required?

c) What impact could these issues have on your commitment to the process?

d) When you think about all the issues above in all the questions, what are your views on the emotional resilience that may be needed, and do you think you have this?

We realise that this exercise is likely to have raised a number of concerns for you. For a baby or young child, such a placement provides many positives. It is the adults who take the risks, and we want to be sure that you have thought about the difficulties that might lie ahead. We need to know that you as an individual – or both of you if you are adopting as a couple – have really reflected on what might be involved so that you don't feel pushed into making a decision that does not feel right for you. This leaflet will have raised questions that can be discussed with your social worker and will contribute to the information being incorporated into your PAR.

Adapted with kind permission of Families for Children

Appendix 9
Information for friends, family, employers and colleagues of Fostering for Adoption carers

The following text comes from a leaflet published by CCS Adoption, which is designed to explain FfA for the support network of FfA carers.

Who is this information for?

You may be aware that your friend, colleague or family member has been thinking about adoption for some time. You may understand adoption but not what adopting by FfA means.

If someone you know has chosen to adopt via an FfA route, what does this mean?

This means that they have been assessed and approved as adopters but also as temporary foster carers for a specific child. The plan will be that they will have a child placed with them for whom they will act as foster carers while the court process continues and final decisions are made about the child's future. The local authority will have completed assessments on the birth parents and concluded that they are unable to care safely for the child in the long term. The local authority will also have looked for and assessed any possible wider family members and decided that none are suitable to care for the child. Therefore the local authority will be working solely on a plan of adoption for the child. However, it is important to realise that the courts may not have agreed this plan and it is possible that the court may not agree with the local authority at the final hearing stage. This could mean that further assessments are ordered or that the child could be returned to their birth family.

Why might the child return to their birth family?

Children are best brought up within their own families wherever this is safe and possible and this principle in enshrined in law in the Children Act 1989. Sometimes it can be difficult for birth parents to care for a child and they need additional services to help them meet their needs. For some parents, complex problems and previous parenting histories may prompt the local authority to consider other plans for the child's future at the same time as trying to support change in the birth parents. Local authorities often work on these plans simultaneously. People can sometimes make drastic changes to enable them to care for a child and they must be given every reasonable opportunity to do so, as long as the timescales they are given in which to change also fit with the needs of the child. The courts may take a view that the local authority has not offered enough support to the birth parents, or that they must be given more time to make changes.

Adoption is a very drastic step as it severs the link between the child and their birth family forever. It is clear from statute and case law that adoption should only ever be seen as a last resort after all other options have been properly considered. However, if the social work assessments on the birth parents and the wider family are robust and the options for the child well analysed in the child's care plan, it would not be unreasonable for the local authority to ask the court to agree with their plan.

Why not wait till all the decision-making is over before placing the child with adopters?

Children need a stable and secure permanent home in which to develop and grow. We know from research that being in temporary foster care is harmful to children and any unnecessary moves can cause further disruption and damage. Children need stability and good quality care, especially in their early years in order to form secure attachments to their primary carers. If children develop a secure attachment to their primary carers, this will form their attachment pattern for life. Likewise, if they form insecure or chaotic attachments to their primary carers, it will be very difficult for them to form more functional positive relationships later in life. Therefore, the goal of all child and family social work is to achieve timely permanence for a child, preferably within their birth family, but if this is not possible then within another suitable family. FfA placements enable a child to start living in their permanent home and begin to form secure attachments to their FfA carers as early as possible, avoiding more months of temporary foster care and another disruptive move to their adopters after the granting of a placement order as, if the court agrees with the local authority that adoption is the right plan for the child, the child will already be settled in their permanent adoptive home.

Isn't this asking a lot of FfA carers?

Yes, you are right, it is. However, we believe that the sooner a child is placed in their permanent adoptive home (if that is their plan), the better. Some adopters will also be keen to offer a child the stability of permanence as soon as possible and commit to that child from an earlier stage in their lives and their care journey. Your friend, colleague or family member will have been carefully assessed and prepared to undertake this role. They will also be well supported by their social worker. If you are very closely involved in this journey as a prospective adoptive grandparent or aunt/uncle, hopefully you will have been given the opportunity to attend an information session or some training yourselves. However, don't worry if this hasn't happened, as it should still be possible for you to have a chance to talk to your family member's social worker. Please contact your local authority directly.

How can I help the carer?

Being an FfA carer is demanding and people undertaking this role will need understanding, support and acceptance from those around them. Below is a checklist of points that may be helpful. But remember – everyone is different so it may be best for you to check out with them what they would find helpful.

- Remember that the child they have living with them *is not their adopted child* but a child they are acting as *foster carers* for.
- Decide up front with the carers what they want you to tell other people about what is happening: what story do they want you to tell?
- Be perceptive about what they may need your help with – work out what you can do for them and consult with them.
- Encourage them to ask for help but also offer it so that they don't have to do the asking.
- Provide them with practical support such as cleaning, cooking and shopping.
- Have a balanced approach to their situation, as there is a chance that the child will not remain with them. It is therefore not helpful to be too gushing!
- Find ways to manage your own emotions and be balanced around the carers. Think about how you will achieve this before they have a child placed with them.
- Try not to ask questions about the long term, such as which school or nursery the child will attend.
- Accept that the carers may not be as available to you as they were in the past.

- Be flexible, listen and provide reassurance.
- From time to time, remind them why they decided to become FfA carers.
- Gently help them to stay focused on the best interests of the child.
- Help them get through on a day-to-day basis rather than looking too far ahead.
- Provide them with affirmation, not criticism.
- Help them to appreciate even small things, for example, enjoying the child's milestones and first experiences.
- Spread the word about what you have learnt or know about FfA to the rest of the support network.
- Provide the carers with a break by going for a walk with them and the baby, or by being in their home so that you can make them tea or play with the baby.
- The carers will have been told not to refer to themselves as "Mummy" and "Daddy" but to use first names. It would help for you to do this too.
- Please remember that the child has birth parents and is still in a relationship with them while assessments continue.
- FfA carers have found it very upsetting to have people congratulate them on becoming a "mummy" or a "daddy" when they hear that a child is living with them. Please refrain from doing this.
- Because the child the carers have living with them is in the care system, confidentiality is important and they may not be able to share much information with you. Please understand this.
- When the child is first placed with them, your friend, colleague or family member will be focusing on helping the child to build a secure attachment to them. This will mean that they may not seem very sociable and you may feel pushed away. Please understand this in terms of the task they have taken on; the child is not "theirs" and it would not be good for the child's development at this stage to have contact with lots of different people.
- Being an FfA carer is challenging. Just "being there" for your friend, colleague or family member can be a great support. Listening, but not asking lots of questions or giving your own opinions can help.
- Your friend, colleague or family member may themselves be struggling with very strong feelings at times. If you have strong feelings triggered by this process, try to get support for yourself so that you don't end up burdening the carer with your feelings to cope with as well.
- If people wish to send a card or gift, send it to the child who can take it with them if they leave.

- Please don't buy "Congratulations on your new baby" cards.
- When talking to the child, refer to yourselves by your first name – you are not the child's Granny/Grandpa/Auntie, etc.
- Remember that your friend, colleague or family member has chosen to care for a child in this manner and been assessed and prepared to do so. It can help to have and show confidence in them and their coping abilities.

If the court agrees with the local authority that the child's birth parents are not able to provide a safe and secure future home, and that adoption is the plan for the child, they will make a full care order and placement order in court. It is at this stage that your friend, colleague or family member can begin to think about themselves as the child's prospective adoptive parent. However, if the adoption is contested by the birth parents, they may still have a long journey ahead of them until they have an adoption order and the appeal period has expired.

If you have questions about anything in this information sheet, contact your local authority adoption/fostering team and ask to talk to someone about FfA, or visit www.first4adoption.org.uk.

Reproduced with kind permission of CCS Adoption

Appendix 10
Fostering for Adoption Carer Agreement

(Fostering Services Regulations 2011, Reg. 27(5)(a) and (b)

This Agreement, dated ____________, is between ______________________ Council and approved Fostering for Adoption carer/s:

____

1. **Terms of approval**

   You are approved as temporary foster carers by ______________________ Council's Nominated Officer to provide a placement for:

   ______________________________ **under Regulation 25a of the Care Planning, Placement And Case Review (England) (Miscellaneous Amendments) Regulations 2013**

2. You will have a named adoption social worker who will visit you at least every two weeks and who will contact you by phone in the intervening weeks.

   In accordance with Standard 21 (Fostering Services National Minimum Standards), you will receive at least one unannounced visit annually.

   Your adoption social worker is: ______________________

3. Your approval as temporary foster carers will be for a specific child to be placed with you as part of the Fostering for Adoption scheme and will be managed and reviewed by the adoption service.

4. You will be advised of any changes to the council's policies and procedures and legislative governance relating to your role as family placement carers.

5. You are only approved to care for the specific child/ren named in section 1 of this agreement and must not allow yourself to be approached by anyone else to accept a placement.

6. When placing a child or young person in your home on a Fostering for Adoption basis, the Children's Services department will provide you with the appropriate Child in Care (CiC) paperwork and:

- financial arrangements for the support of the child during the placement;
- arrangements for the delegation of responsibility for consent to the medical or dental examination or treatment of the child;
- arrangements for obtaining approval from Children's Services for the child to live, even temporarily, away from your home. This includes holidays, school trips and visits to your own extended family;
- arrangements for meeting the medical, educational, safety and social needs of the child.

The above matters will normally be addressed during the Pre-Placement Planning Meeting, that must occur prior to all placements or on the next working day in respect of emergency or immediate placements.

7. The Adoption Service undertakes to support this placement by ensuring that:

- agreed financial allowances are paid promptly;
- you are provided with adequate supervision;
- you have appropriate agreed access to advice and consultation with allied professional services;
- you have appropriate access to peer support;
- "enhanced" support is provided promptly if/when a placement or aspects of a placement result or are likely to result in unusual or unacceptable strain on your normal family circumstances.

As temporary foster carer/s, you are required:

8. To give immediate/written notice to the Adoption Service, with full particulars of:

- any intended change of your address;
- any change in the composition of the household;
- any criminal offence for which you or a member of your immediate family has been found guilty or any other change in the/your circumstances which may affect your ability to care for a child placed or the suitability of your household;
- any request or application to adopt children, apply for special guardianship, a child arrangements order or for registration for childminding or day care.

9. Not to administer corporal punishment to any child placed with you.

10. To ensure that any information relating to a child placed with you, to the child's family or to any other person, which has been given to you in confidence in connection with a placement, is kept confidential and is not disclosed to any person without the consent of the Adoption Service.

11. To return any written information appertaining to the placement to the Adoption Service at the conclusion of the placement or at any time the Adoption Service considers appropriate.

12. To comply with the terms of any Adoption Service Agreement in respect of children/young people placed in your home.

This will include promotion of the child's education and a requirement not to remove the child from their education setting during term times to facilitate family holidays unless this is in very exceptional circumstances and not without the express permission of the Senior Manager responsible for the child's case management.

13. To care for any child placed with you as if the child were a member of your own family and to promote their welfare, having regard to the long- and short-term plans for the child and having due regard for appropriate safe care practices at all times.

14. To keep ______________________ Council's Children's Services department informed about the child's progress and to notify them immediately of any significant events affecting the child.

15. To safeguard any child placed with you from abuse or neglect, and in circumstances where an allegation of abuse or neglect is made, to co-operate with the local authority's policies and procedures for the investigation and conduct of such matters.

16. To allow any child placed with you to be removed from your home if the Directorate of Services for Children, Schools and Families considers that the continuation of a placement would be detrimental to the welfare of the child or if the placement is no longer considered the most suitable way of meeting the child's assessed needs.

17. In such circumstances where you require an unplanned and premature termination of the placement of any child in your care, that you will give a minimum of 28 days' notice to the Adoption Service of your requirement for the end of any such placement.

In such circumstances, the Family Placement Service will consider the welfare and security of any child in placement to be paramount but will have due regard and sensitivity for any reasonable request from you as a family placement carer.

18. *You should be clear that it is possible this placement may not lead to adoption, for example, because the local authority's plan changes and ______________________ can be safely returned to his or her birth parents' care; or because a friend or family member comes forward to care for him or her; or because the court does not grant a placement order; or because* *the local authority does not agree to you being matched with the child for adoption.*

Signed (Fostering for Adoption carer)

Print name:

Date:

Signed (Fostering for Adoption carer)

Print name:

Date:

Signed: (Adoption service manager)

Print name:

Date:

Reproduced with kind permission of Cornwall Council